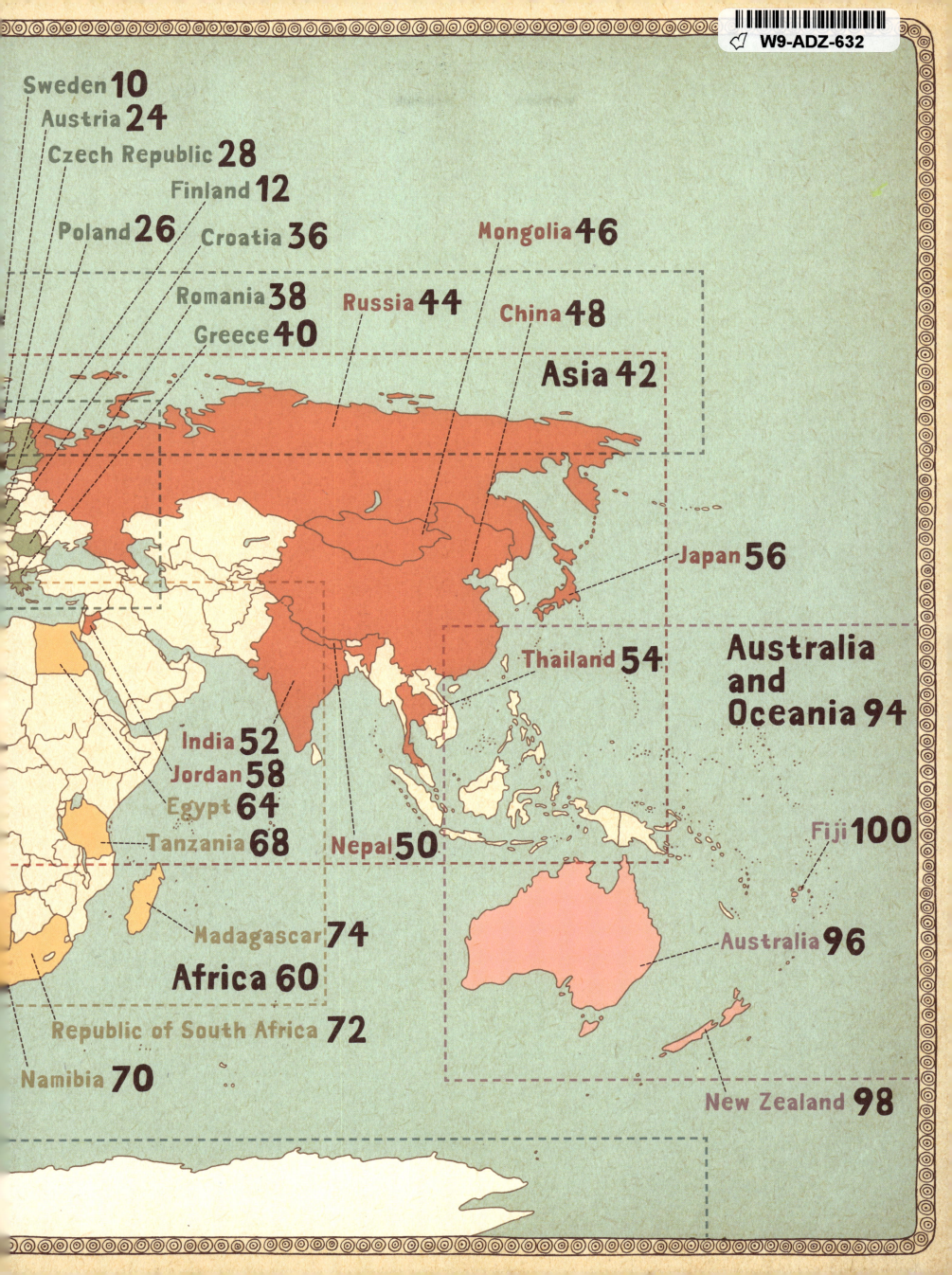

Sweden **10**
Austria **24**
Czech Republic **28**
Finland **12**
Poland **26** Croatia **36**
Mongolia **46**
Romania **38** Russia **44**
Greece **40** China **48**

Asia **42**

Japan **56**

Thailand **54**

Australia
and
Oceania **94**

India **52**
Jordan **58**
Egypt **64**
Tanzania **68** Nepal **50**

Fiji **100**

Madagascar **74**

Australia **96**

Africa **60**

Republic of South Africa **72**

Namibia **70**

New Zealand **98**

MAPS

Aleksandra Mizielińska and Daniel Mizieliński

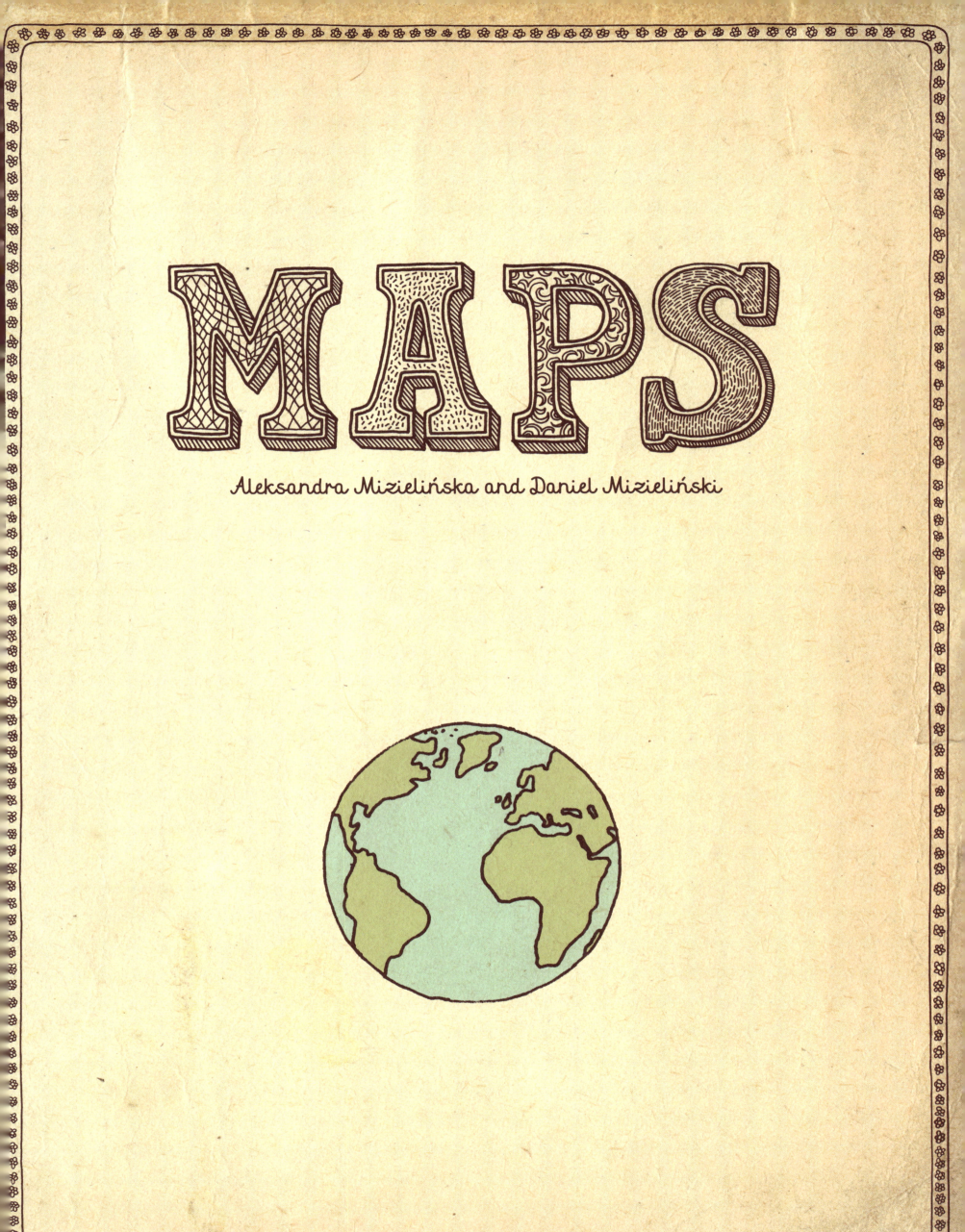

WORLD

NORTH
WEST · EAST
SOUTH

THE ARCTIC

GRAY SEAL

OCEAN LINER

EUROPE

NORTH AMERICA

ATLANTIC OCEAN

AFRICA

ORCA

PACIFIC OCEAN

PIRATE SHIP

GIANT TORTOISE

SOUTH AMERICA

RAY

SPERM WHALE

DOLPHINS

SUBMARINE

SOUTHERN OCEAN

4

MAP

ARCTIC OCEAN

ASIA

PACIFIC OCEAN

INDIAN OCEAN

SEA TURTLE

SHARK

SAILING SHIP

AUSTRALIA

OCEANIA

HAMMERHEAD SHARK

BLUE WHALE

CONTAINER SHIP

ANTARCTICA

SOWERBY'S
BEAKED WHALE

REYKJAVÍK
ICELAND

GRAY
SEAL

HARBOR
PORPOISE

NORTH ATLANTIC
RIGHT WHALE

Faroe
Islands
(Denmark)

NORWAY

Shetland Islands
(United Kingdom)

OSLO

SPINY LOBSTER

NORTH SEA

ATLANTIC
HERRING

DAB

DUBLIN
IRELAND

DENMARK

COPENHAGEN

SEI WHALE

UNITED
KINGDOM

LONDON

AMSTERDAM
NETHERLANDS

GERMANY

BERLIN

ATLANTIC COD

BRUSSELS
BELGIUM

LUXEMBOURG

LUXEMBOURG

PRAGUE

CZECH
REPUB

A T L A N T I C   O C E A N

PARIS

FRANCE

LIECHTENSTEIN

VADUZ

VIENN

MACKEREL

BERN

SWITZERLAND

AUSTRIA

EUROPEAN
PILCHARD

SLOVENIA

LJUBLJAN

ITALY

CROATI

PORTUGAL

ANDORRA

MONACO
MONACO

VATICAN CITY

SAN
MARINO

SAN MARINO

MADRID

ANDORRA
LA VELLA

Corsica
(France)

ROME

BLUEFIN TUNA

LISBON

SPAIN

Balearic Islands
(Spain)

SEA URCHIN

Sardinia (Italy)

JOHN DORY

MEDITERRANEAN
SEA

MEDITERRANEAN
MORAY

Sicily (Italy)

VALLETT

6

EUROPE

47 COUNTRIES

POPULATION: 740 MILLION

SIZE: 10,354,636 KM²/ 3,997,929 SQ. MI.

0 100 200 300 400 500 kilometers
0 50 100 150 200 250 miles

Part of the agreed border between Europe and Asia runs through the Ural Mountains.

BARENTS SEA

WHITE SEA

SWEDEN

FINLAND

LAKE ONEGA

LAKE LADOGA

HELSINKI

STOCKHOLM

BALTIC SEA

TALLINN
ESTONIA

LAKE PEIPUS

RUSSIA

MOSCOW

Gotland

RIGA
LATVIA

LITHUANIA

VILNIUS

MINSK

Only part of Kazakhstan is in Europe.

KALININGRAD OBLAST (RUSSIA)

POLAND

BELARUS

KAZAKHSTAN

WARSAW

KIEV

UKRAINE

SLOVAKIA
BRATISLAVA

HUNGARY

MOLDOVA
CHIŞINĂU

BUDAPEST

SEA OF AZOV

STURGEON

ROMANIA

BLACK SEA

CASPIAN SEA

BELGRADE

BUCHAREST

SNIA D GOVINA
AJEVO

SERBIA

BULGARIA

SEA HORSE

HERMIT CRAB

MONTENEGRO
PRISTINA
KOSOVO

ODGORICA

SOFIA

SKOPJE

MACEDONIA

ALBANIA

TIRANA

TURKEY

ANKARA

GREECE

ATHENS

*TURKEY
Only a small part of Turkey is in Europe.*

SQUID

Crete (Greece)

Rhodes (Greece)

ATLANTIC HALIBUT

HORNSTRANDIR NATURE RESERVE

GREENLAND SEA

HADDOCK

ÍSAFJÖRÐUR

GREENLAND SHARK

THICK-BILLE MURRE

ARCTIC FOX

GYRFALCON

BLUEBERRIES

JUNIPER

HVÍTSERKUR CLIFF

SAUÐÁRKRÓKUR

TURF HOUSE

GRAY SEAL

ICELANDIC HORSE

CROWBERRIES

CYCLING

GREAT BLACK-BACKED GULL

SHEEP

DEILDARTUNGUHVER hot spring

RAFTING

Langjökull Glacier

SNÆFELLSJÖKULL VOLCANO
The summit of the volcano is covered by a glacier.

SHEEP'S WOOL SWEATER

ATLANTIC WOLFFISH

LIGHTHOUSE

ÞINGVELLIR NATIONAL PARK

SKYR
a kind of yogurt

AKRANES

CATHEDRAL

STROKKUR GEYSER
sends water up 30 meters / 100 feet

HEKLA VOLCANO

RÚGBRAUÐ
sweet rye bread

KLEINA
fried pastry

REYKJAVÍK
KÓPAVOGUR
HAFNARFJÖRÐUR

POTATOES

KEFLAVÍK

SELFOSS

ÞJÓRSÁ

HAY

ÞORRAMATUR

BATHING IN THE BLUE LAGOON
a pool filled with water from hot springs

EYJAFJALLAJÖKULL VOLCANO

a selection of traditional Icelandic delicacies, mainly made of meat and fish

HANDBALL

ATLANTIC OCEAN

Heimaey

HEIMAEY

8

WHALE WATCHING

EUROPEAN PLAICE

ROCK PTARMIGAN

PORT

HÚSAVÍK

DETTIFOSS WATERFALL

WILLOW

CAPELIN

BLUE WHITING

ROWANBERRIES

AKUREYRI

WHOOPER SWAN

HEATHER

REINDEER

GRAYLAG GOOSE

HIKING

SKIER

SKJÁLFANDAFLJÓT

HERÐUBREIÐ
extinct volcano

EGILSSTAÐIR

JÖKULSÁ Á DAL

LINGONBERRIES

ATLANTIC PUFFIN

GLACIER

ICELAND MOSS

ASKJA VOLCANO

JÖKULSÁ Á FJÖLLUM

JÖKULSÁ Í FLJÓTSDAL

Hofsjökull Glacier

BÁRÐARBUNGA VOLCANO

MALLARD

Vatnajökull Glacier
Iceland's biggest glacier

LANDMANNALAUGAR

SVARTIFOSS WATERFALL

HVANNADALSHNÚKUR
2,109 meters / 6,952 ft.
Iceland's highest peak

Ísland
↑
the country's name in Icelandic

ÓLAFUR

ANÍTA

LAKI VOLCANO

0   25   50 kilometers
0   25 miles

CRANBERRY FLOWERS

CRANBERRIES

Mýrdalsjökull Glacier

ICELANDERS IN TRADITIONAL COSTUMES

ICELAND

CAPITAL: REYKJAVÍK

LANGUAGE: ICELANDIC

POPULATION: 320,000

AREA: 103,000 KM²/ 40,000 SQ. MI.

KATLA VOLCANO

BIRCH

9

SWEDEN

Sverige the country's name in Swedish

🏔️ CAPITAL: STOCKHOLM

🍄 LANGUAGE: SWEDISH

👤 POPULATION: 9 MILLION

🧭 AREA: 450,295 KM²/ 173,860 SQ. MI.

kilometers
0 25 50 75 100
miles
0   25   50

THE SAMI PEOPLE live in the far north

REINDEER

NORTHERN HAWK-OWL

WOLF

BROWN BEAR

NORTHERN LAPWING

ROE DEER

LYNX

PINE

WOOD GROUSE

ICEBREAKER

GULF OF BOTHNIA

ICE HOTEL

IRON ORE EXTRACTION

TORNE

LULE

WILLOW PTARMIGAN

ARCTIC CIRCLE
→ See explanation on page 12.

KIRUNA ①

KEBNEKAISE
2,113 metres / 6,936 ft.,
Sweden's highest peak

ABISKO NATIONAL PARK ①

GAMMELSTAD
pilgrims' village

LULEÅ

SKELLEFTE

SKELLEFTEÅ

WOODEN HOUSES

UME

UMEÅ

KUNGSLEDEN
hiking trail

TAIGA
coniferous forest that grows
all over the north of Europe,
Asia, and America

SKULESKOGEN
NATIONAL PARK

SUNDSVALL

TIMBER PRODUCTION

ÅNGERMAN

BROWN TROUT

INDALS

ELK

DYNAMITE

ALFRED NOBEL
invented dynamite
and founded the
Nobel Prize

CABLE CAR

ÅRE

SKIING

CROSS-COUNTRY SKIING

WOOD LEMMING

PIPPI

ASTRID LINDGREN
author of the Pippi Longstocking books

RAFTING

MOUNTAIN HARE

CAMPING

CARP

CYCLING TOURS

EUROPEAN EEL

FISHING

EBBA   HUGO

VIKING
Scandinavian
sailor and
warrior

VIKING BOAT

CARL LINNAEUS
botanist and zoologist

INGMAR BERGMAN
film director

SWEDISH NATIONAL COSTUME

COMMON EIDER

EUROPEAN BEAVER

CRAYFISH

VELVET DUCK

EUROPEAN HONEY BUZZARD

DANCING AROUND THE MAYPOLE at the summer solstice festival

CANDLE WREATH worn by girls on SAINT LUCIA'S DAY

ANDERS CELSIUS
Physicist and astronomer invented the temperature scale known as the Celsius scale

ATLANTIC SALMON

RUNIC STONE one of many found near Uppsala

CASTLE

DAL

ROYAL CASTLE

STACKS rock formations

Farö

BALTIC SEA

BARLEY

Gotland

ATLANTIC HERRING

UPPSALA

STOCKHOLM

HOUSES ON STORTORGET HISTORICAL MARKET SQUARE

FORTIFICATIONS

Øsund

VISBY

GÄVLE

OATS

DALECARLIAN HORSE

Sveaeland

LAKE MÄLAREN

LAKE HJÄLMAREN

CASTLE

ÖREBRO

CHICKEN FARMING

JÖNKÖPING

KALMAR CASTLE

KALMAR

PIG FARMING

NUSNÄS

WATER TOWER

KARLSTAD

LAKE VÄNERN

LAKE VÄTTERN

RAPESEED

SUGAR BEETS

Götaland

BORÅS

WHEAT

TOWN HALL

HELSINGBORG

MALMÖ

BRIDGE ACROSS ØRESUND STRAIT linking Denmark and Sweden

LUSSEKATT a sweet bun with saffron and raisins

FIKA a coffee break

YACHT

GOTHENBURG

KATTEGAT

TOWN HALL

KÖTTBULLAR meatballs served with potatoes and lingonberry jam

GRAVLAX salmon marinated in salt, sugar and dill

MUSEUM OF ART AND POSEIDON STATUE ON GÖTAPLATSEN SQUARE

SKAGERRAK

ICE HOCKEY

SMÖRGÅSBORD

BLÅBÄRSSOPPA a soup made of blueberries

NYPONSOPPA a soup made of wild rose hips

BILBERRY JAM

THREE CROWNS national emblem of Sweden

ROYAL GUARDSMAN

⊘

11

FINLAND

Suomi the country's name in Finnish

🏳️ CAPITAL: HELSINKI

🗣️ LANGUAGES: FINNISH, SWEDISH

👥👥👥 POPULATION: 5 MILLION

📐 AREA: 338,145 KM²/ 130,559 SQ. MI.

Finland the country's name in Swedish

In winter the ERMINE's coat turns white.

RIDING A SNOWMOBILE

BROWN BEAR

WOLF

WOLVERINE

hiking on the BEAR'S RING trail

OULANKA NATIONAL PARK

FIR

PINES

ASH

BIRCH

OAK

BIRCH LEAF

MAPLE LEAF

In winter its coat turns white.

MOUNTAIN HARE

TUNDRA a treeless area where mosses and lichen grow due to the cold climate

LAKE INARI

LEMMENJOKI NATIONAL PARK

REINDEER

REINDEER LICHEN

traditional SAMI tent

WOOD LEMMING

HALTIATUNTURI 1,328 meters/4,343 ft. Finland's highest point

SUOMI-NEITO the Maiden of Finland

The Finns love SAUNAS.

DWARF BIRCH

VÄINÄMÖINEN mythical hero, god, and wizard

KANTELE folk instrument

SLED-DOG TEAM

ELK

SNOWY OWL

PORTTIPAHTA RESERVOIR

LOKKA RESERVOIR

REINDEER FARMING

LEVI ski resort

SKIER

KYTÄKYNTTILÄ BRIDGE

SANTA CLAUS VILLAGE

KIANTAJÄRVI

CALYPSO ORCHID

● ROVANIEMI ②

KEMIJÄRVI

TAIGA

PAPER MANUFACTURE

KEMIJOKI

the world's biggest SNOW CASTLE

LAKE YLI-KÄITÄ

statue of a policeman in Oulu's marketplace

TORIPOLLIISI

● KEMI

ARCTIC CIRCLE

① As many as 21 hydro-electric power stations have been built along the Kemijoki.

This region of Finland is known as the ARM.

The shape of Finland resembles a person stretching out an arm.

THE SAMI people live in Lapland.

WHOOPER SWAN

② SANTA CLAUS apparently lives in the town of Rovaniemi.

NORDIC WALKING, or hiking with poles, was invented in Finland.

WOOD GROUSE

CUCKOO

① North of the Arctic Circle, in winter there are POLAR NIGHTS when the sun does not rise above the horizon for many days or weeks on end. In summer, during POLAR DAYS, the sun is visible above the horizon 24 hours a day.

composer JEAN SIBELIUS

ASH LEAF

WHORTLEBERRIES
CLOUDBERRIES
RASPBERRIES
ROWANBERRIES
SEA BUCKTHORN
BLUEBERRIES
RYE BREAD
SALMIAKKI — licorice flavored with ammonium chloride
MEATBALLS with potatoes and lingonberry jam
KARELIAN PASTIES
The Finns drink a lot of COFFEE.

GRAY ALDER
ALDER LEAF
CRANBERRIES

FISHING

LINGONBERRIES

OLAVINLINNA

EUROPEAN PERCH
VENDACE
RUNEBERG'S TORTE — with raspberry jam
PULLA
sweet bread

RINGED SEAL

LEIPÄJUUSTO — cheese made of cow's milk or reindeer milk and served with jam

PEA SOUP

LAKE LENTUA

JOENSUU
LAKE ORIVESI

LAKE PIELINEN
KAYAKER

SAVONLINNA
LAKE PIHLAJAVESI
LAKE PIHLAJAVESI

IMATRA

OULUJÄRVI
KAJAANI

BOLETUS EDULIS

NEW VALAMO MONASTERY

LAKE HAUKIVESI
MIKKELI

RINGED SEAL

SUOMENLINNA — sea fortress

Lake District

KUOPIO
LAKE KALLAVESI
SKATER

LAKE SAIMAA
LAPPEENRANTA
KOUVOLA

KOTKA

OULUJOKI
CHANTERELLES

JYVÄSKYLÄ
YACHT
SKI JUMPING
OLD TOWN
PORVOO

GULF OF FINLAND

LAKE KEITELE
CROSS-COUNTRY SKIER

Finland

LAKE PÄIJÄNNE

LAHTI

GULF OF BOTHNIA

FORESTS cover a large part of Finland.

The Finns use WOOD to make paper and furniture, and also to build houses.

NÄSINNEULA observation tower
CATHEDRAL
TAMPERE
HÄME CASTLE
HÄMEENLINNA
CATHEDRAL
VANTAA
HELSINKI
ESPOO

VAASA

RYE
SUGAR BEETS
RAPESEED
WHEAT

CATHEDRAL
TURKU

BARLEY
OATS

TOWN HALL
PORI
MOOMIN HOUSE
RAUMA
NAANTALI

CASTLE

PESÄPALLO — Finnish baseball

TOVE JANSSON author of the Moomin books

WOODEN HOUSES IN OLD RAUMA

SALMON

ALVAR AALTO architect and designer

VEETI

ATLANTIC HERRING

KASTELHOLM — medieval castle

Åland Islands

BALTIC SEA

AINO

TUFTED DUCK

MARIEHAMN

13

CRICKET

GOLF

CHICKEN TIKKA MASALA
chicken marinated with spices and yogurt, served in a cream and tomato sauce

FISH AND CHIPS

TENNIS

SUNDAY ROAST
roast meat, potatoes, vegetables, and Yorkshire pudding

HORSE RACING

FULL ENGLISH BREAKFAST

Shetland Islands

ATLANTIC OCEAN

LERWICK
SHETLAND PONY

Orkney Islands

THE STANDING STONES of Stenness

KIRKWALL

NORTH SEA

RUGBY

BADMINTON

NORTH SEA

CASTLE

NEWCASTLE UPON TYNE

MICKLEGATE B

MOORLANDS

SOCCER

ABERDEEN

PING-PONG

EUROPEAN HEDGEHOG

TYNE BRIDGE

The British are famous for their luxury CARS.

the legendary LOCH NESS MONSTER

SCOTSMAN playing the BAGPIPES

KILT
a traditional Scotsman's garment

GRAMPIAN MOUNTAINS

CASTLE

EDINBURGH

SHEEP FARMING

LAKE DISTRICT

S c o t l a n d

SCOTCH WHISKEY

LOCH NESS

BEN NEVIS
1,343 meters, 4,406 ft., the United Kingdom's highest peak

CLYDE AUDITORIUM CONCERT HALL

GLASGOW

CLYDE ARC BRIDGE

RED FOX

RED DEER

NORTHWEST HIGHLANDS

Skye

Rhum

Coll

Tree

North Uist

South Uist

Mull

Arran

Islay

H e b r i d e s

Isle of Lewis

CASTLE

BELFAST

GIANT'S CAUSEWAY

DERRY

LOUGH NEAGH

Northern Ireland

ISAAC NEWTON
mathematician, physicist, and astronomer

SHERLOCK HOLMES
the detective from novels by Sir Arthur Conan Doyle

According to legend, ROBIN HOOD lived in SHERWOOD FOREST.

PETER PAN
hero of the book by J.M. Barrie

14

ENGLISH GENTLEMAN

YORKSHIRE PUDDING baked pastry made of water, flour, eggs, and milk

WHEAT

POTATOES

SUGAR BEETS

BARLEY

UNIVERSITY

CAMBRIDGE

BIG BEN

PALACE OF WESTMINSTER

LONDON EYE

LONDON

THAMES

WHITE CLIFFS

DOVER

THE ENGLISH CHANNEL

QUEEN ELIZABETH II

ROYAL GUARDSMAN

LONDON TELEPHONE BOX

LONDON BUS

BODIAM CASTLE

YORK

LEEDS

TOWN HALL

SHEFFIELD

MANCHESTER

PEAK DISTRICT NATIONAL PARK

SHERWOOD FOREST ①

BULL RING shopping center

BIRMINGHAM

TOWER BRIDGE

OXFORD

UNIVERSITY

②

STONEHENGE

Isle of Wight

UFFINGTON WHITE HORSE a huge outline of a horse carved into the hillside thousands of years ago

②

LIBRARY

LIVERPOOL

CHARLES DARWIN established the theory of evolution

SEVERN

CATTLE FARMING

BRISTOL

BLACKPOOL TOWER

ROYAL LIVER BUILDING

CASTLE

WALES MILLENNIUM CENTRE

IN THESE STONES HORIZONS SING

CARDIFF

CAMBRIAN MOUNTAINS

WEOBLEY CASTLE

KING ARTHUR legendary sixth-century ruler

BRITISH BULLDOG

IRISH SEA

Anglesey

CAERNARFON CASTLE

RED KITE

The Isle of Man is a dependency of the United Kingdom but has its own government.

ALICE, heroine of Lewis Carroll's books

CELTIC SEA

Afternoon TEA is a British tradition.

THE BEATLES

CHARLIE CHAPLIN actor and film director

WILLIAM SHAKESPEARE poet and playwright

JACK

OLIVIA

United Kingdom

CAPITAL: LONDON

LANGUAGES: ENGLISH as well as Welsh, Scots, Irish, Scottish, Gaelic, and Cornish.

POPULATION: 63 MILLION

AREA: 243,610 KM²/ 94,058 SQ. MI.

0 25 50 kilometers
0 25 miles

15

NETHERLANDS

Nederland ← the country's name in Dutch

♛ CAPITAL: AMSTERDAM

🍄 LANGUAGES: DUTCH and Frisian

👨‍👧‍👦 POPULATION: 17 MILLION

↔ AREA: 41,543 KM²/ 16,040 SQ. MI.

LIEKE STIJN

BLACK WOODPECKER

NATURAL GAS EXTRACTION

BARLEY

POTATOES

ERMINE

MOUFLONS live in De Hoge Veluwe Nat'l Park ③

ENSCHEDE

GROTE KERK

HUIS BERGH CASTLE

PREHISTORIC TOMBS

Groningen UNIVERSITY

GRONINGEN

ASSEN

Drenthe

GIETHOORN VILLAGE

CATTLE FARMING

COMMON SHELDUCK

LEEUWARDEN

Friesland

Overijssel

IJssel

HET LOO PALACE AND GARDENS

ZWOLLE

Gelderland

Castle at Ruurlo

ARNHEM

CAROLINGIAN CHAPEL

Ameland

Schiermonnikoog

Rottumerplaat

Rottumeroog

walking on the seabed at low tide

HIKING

MUDFLAT

PIED AVOCET

WADDENZEE

MERGANSER

SCHOKLAND An abandoned settlement that was once on an island ①

DE HOGE VELUWE NATIONAL PARK ③

APELDOORN

LELYSTAD

Flevoland

ALMERE

CATHEDRAL

UTRECHT

RHINE

Utrecht

North Holland

OYSTERCATCHER

HOUSES ON THE AMSTERDAM CANALS

VOLENDAM

AMSTERDAM

KEUKENHOF FLOWER GARDEN

GOUDA Rotterdam is Europe's biggest port.

Texel

Wieringen

LIGHTHOUSE

BEACH

ZAANSE SCHANS

Trompur windmill

Orupour windmill

WINDMILL MUSEUM

HAARLEM

LEIDEN

THE HAGUE

South Holland

DELFT

ROTTERDAM

NIEUWE KERK

RIDDERZAAL

LESSER BLACK-BACKED GULL

kilometers
0 5 10 15 20 25
0   5   10 miles

ATLANTIC HERRING

N O R T H   S E A

SOLE

THE WINDMILLS IN SCHIEDAM ARE THE TALLEST IN THE WORLD.

16

RED DEER

FLOWER MARKET

TULIP-BULB SELLER

THE DUTCH LOVE TO RIDE BICYCLES.

ROOKWORST
smoked sausage

ONTBIJTKOEK
breakfast cake

GOUDA CHEESE

BABY LONG-EARED OWLS

LONG-EARED OWL

STAMPPOT
mashed potatoes with vegetables

ERWTENSOEP
pea soup

EDAM CHEESE

DAFFODILS

HYACINTHS

VLA
a dessert made of milk, eggs, vanilla, and sugar

VAALSERBERG
322 metres / 1,056 ft., the highest point in the European part of the Netherlands

PIET MONDRIAN
painter

The Netherlands governs several islands in the Caribbean (see page 76).

DELFT PORCELAIN

MAAS

SUGAR BEETS

Limburg

CORN

CITY GATE

MAASTRICHT

VINCENT VAN GOGH
painter

THE MERMAID
from a painting by Vermeer

WOODEN CLOGS

BLUETHROAT

EVOLUON CONFERENCE CENTER

EINDHOVEN

FIERLJEPPEN
a traditional sport

The Netherlands is crisscrossed by many CANALS.

ORANGE is regarded as the traditional color of the Dutch royal family.

JAN VERMEER
painter

North Brabant

TILBURG

② WINDMILLS AT KINDERDIJK

DUTCH PEOPLE CELEBRATING KING'S DAY

REMBRANDT
painter and draftsman

BREDA

WHEAT

SPEED SKATING

DUTCH PEOPLE IN TRADITIONAL COSTUMES
from the town of Volendam

Schouwen-Duiveland

IJoere-Overflakee

SOCCER

TULIP BULBS

① For centuries the Dutch have been DRAINING THE LAND. In many places where there are now towns and arable land, there was once sea.

permanently drained areas that lie below sea level and are used as arable land.

POLDERS

SEA

SEA LEVEL

The Netherlands is a lowland country, a large part of which lies below sea level.

LAND LYING BELOW SEA LEVEL

CHEESE SELLERS

Zeeland

WATER RAIL

MIDDELBURG

a dike protecting from flooding

OOSTERSCHELDE

TULIPS

17

NORTH SEA

350-meter / 1,000 foot long PIER

BEACH

HISTORIC HOUSES ON THE MARKET SQUARE

BLANKENBERGE

BRUGGE

YELLOW-LEGGED GULL

the world's biggest center for polishing DIAMONDS

HISTORIC HOUSES ON THE MARKET SQUARE

POLDERS

BLACK-TAILED GODWIT

HISTORIC BUILDINGS

PORT

ANTWERP

IJZER

GHENT ①

SCHELDE

F l a n d

PEREGRINE FALCON

LEIE

SCHELDE

GRANDE PLACE market square

BRUSSELS ②③

a cow of the BELGIAN BLUE breed

BARLEY

PONT DES TROUS

WATERLOO

BUTTE DU LION

BEGUINES a women's religious community that no longer exists

BEGUINES' HOUSE ①

SINGE DU GRAND GARDE figure of a monkey

BEFFROI watchtower ⑤

BRUSSELS SPROUTS

TOURNAI

MONS ④

CHARLEROI ⑥

BOAT LIFT ON THE CANAL DU CENTRE

④

probably first cultivated within the territory of present-day Belgium

MANNEKEN PIS a fountain in the shape of a boy peeing ②

HIGHER-UP CANAL

LIFTS transport boats between canals built at different levels.

LOWER-DOWN CANAL

THE ATOMIUM a model of an iron crystal 100 meters / 335 feet high ③

GILLE traditional costume of people taking part in the carnival at Binche

GILLE IN A HAT MADE OF OSTRICH FEATHERS ⑥

CASTLE AT CHIMAY

FLOWER CARPET IN BRUSSELS'S MARKET SQUARE

0 5 10 15 20 25 kilometers
0 5 10 miles

NATHAN

ELISE

BRUSSELS GRIFFON

BELGIAN HORSE

BEGONIAS

ADOLPHE SAX invented the saxophone

The first man to propose the theory that the universe started with the Big Bang

Belgium

Belgique ← the country's name in French

👑 CAPITAL: BRUSSELS

👅 LANGUAGES: DUTCH, FRENCH, GERMAN

België the country's name in Dutch

👤👤👤 POPULATION: 11 MILLION

Belgien the country's name in German

AREA: 30,528 KM² / 11,787 SQ. MI.

GEORGES LEMAÎTRE

THE BIG BANG

SAXOPHONE

POTATOES

CANALS connect Belgium's rivers.

MOULES-FRITES
mussels with French fries

WAFFLES

CHOCOLATE SHOP

BEER

CHOCOLATES

WATERZOOI
thick soup with chicken or fish and vegetables

FRITES

WHEAT

painter JAN VAN EYCK

RED DEER

KESTREL

TOWN HALL

● LOUVAIN

ST. QUENTIN'S CATHEDRAL

● HASSELT

MOUNTAIN BIKING

KINGFISHER

WILD BOAR

SUGAR BEETS

Brussels is the headquarters of the EUROPEAN UNION's most important institutions.

PERRON symbol of Liège

HOHES VENN-EIFEL NATURE PARK

PINE MARTEN

CITADEL

LIÈGE ●

EUROPEAN HEDGEHOG

MEUSE

SIGNAL DE BOTRANGE
694 meters / 2,277 ft., Belgium's highest peak

Painter PIETER BRUEGHEL THE ELDER worked in Brussels for many years.

● NAMUR

HIKING

OURTHE

● DINANT

EUROPEAN RABBIT

Painter ANTHONY VAN DYCK was born in Antwerp.

TOURING THE CAVES AT HAN-SUR-LESSE

FRITERIE

painter ROGIER VAN DER WEYDEN

WOMEN FROM PAINTINGS BY ROGIER VAN DER WEYDEN

FAST-FOOD STALL

CASTLE AT BOUILLON

ST. DONAT'S CHURCH

RENÉ MAGRITTE painter

CHARACTER FROM A PAINTING BY RENÉ MAGRITTE

COLLEGIATE CHURCH OF SAINT GERTRUDE AT NIVELLES

ARLON ●

Many famous CARTOON authors come from Belgium.

⑤

19

HOUSE MARTIN

GERMAN SHEPHERD

ALBERT EINSTEIN physicist $E=mc^2$

REMAINS OF THE BERLIN WALL

PUNTING expedition in the SPREEWALD wetlands

LUSATIA geographical region ①

Saxony

BALTIC SEA

CHALK CLIFFS

Rügen

Usedom

LIGHTHOUSE

BEACHES

ROSTOCK

BEACH CHAIRS were invented in Germany.

ASTRONOMICAL CLOCK AT STRALSUND

SUGAR BEETS

LAKE MÜRITZ

Mecklenburg–Vorpommern

Brandenburg

REICHSTAG parliament building

BERLIN
Berlin

BRANDENBURG GATE

ODER

GHERKINS

ZWINGER PALACE

MEISSEN PORCELAIN

LEIPZIG

MEISSEN

DRESDEN

TIMBER FRAMING a wall with the beams visible

SANSSOUCI PALACE

POTSDAM

BAUHAUS BUILDING

DESSAU

CRADLE designed by Peter Keler at the BAUHAUS MUSEUM

WEIMAR

EISENACH

Thuringia

WERRA

FULDA

HERRENHAUSEN GARDENS

CATHEDRAL

MAGDEBURG

Saxony–Anhalt

LYNXES live in the Harz National Park.

HOLSTEN GATE

Fehmarn

SUBMARINE tour

KIEL

LÜBECK

PORT WAREHOUSES

HAMBURG
Hamburg

HEATHLANDS

HANOVER

Schleswig–Holstein

CONTAINER SHIP

STATUE OF THE MUSICIANS OF BREMEN

BREMEN
Bremen

German chemist Felix Hoffmann is credited with the invention of ASPIRIN.

WESER

THE DANDY-HORSE was a prototype for the bicycle. The rider pushed off with his feet.

OYSTERCATCHER

REDSHANK

PIG FARMING

DACHSHUND

NORTH SEA

GRAY SEAL

THE BROTHERS GRIMM wrote many famous fairy tales, including "SNOW WHITE" and "HANSEL AND GRETEL."

philosopher IMMANUEL KANT

JOHANN WOLFGANG VON GOETHE poet

CANALS

CATTLE FARMING

Lower Saxony

North Rhine-Westphalia

CATHEDRAL

COLOGNE

GODESBURG

ESSEN

DÜSSELDORF

CATHEDRAL

ZOLLVEREIN historic coal mine

RUHR VALLEY industrial area

BLACK COAL

ROCK SALT

RHEINTURM TELECOMMUNICATIONS TOWER

GERMANY

LUSATIAN COSTUME

WEISSWURST *white sausage*

DUMPLINGS

GRILLED SAUSAGES

various kinds of BREAD

BEER STEIN

LUDWIG VAN BEETHOVEN *composer and pianist*

① OBER-LAUSITZ MOUNT.

GREEN WOODPECKER

PUMPERNICKEL

SAUERKRAUT *pickled cabbage*

ROAST PORK

② OKTOBERFEST *beer festival*

BERCHTESGADEN NATIONAL PARK

JOHANN SEBASTIAN BACH *composer*

BROWN HARE

ROE DEER

BOREAL OWL

HAZEL GROUSE

BAVARIAN FOREST

DANUBE

PASSAU

Bavaria

INN

ALPS

GARMISCH-PARTENKIRCHEN

WHEAT

REGENSBURG

HOPS

NEW TOWN HALL ②

MUNICH

SKI JUMPING

GOLDEN EAGLE

SOCCER

NUREMBERG

CASTLE

RYE

ZUGSPITZE 2,963 meters / 9,720 ft. Germany's highest peak

Gutenberg's metal TYPE featuring the letter "ë"

THURINGIAN FOREST

BARLEY

POTATOES

Hesse

MERCEDES-BENZ MUSEUM

PORSCHE

NEUSCHWANSTEIN CASTLE

GUTENBERG BIBLE

Gutenberg built the PRINTING PRESS, which made it possible to print books in large numbers.

RÖMERBERG *marketplace*

SKYSCRAPERS

FRANKFURT AM MAIN

CASTLE

HEIDELBERG

NECKAR

STUTTGART

GRAPEVINES

ULM

LIGHTHOUSE

LAKE CONSTANCE

DEUTSCHLAND *the country's name in German*

JOHANNES GUTENBERG

MARKSBURG CASTLE

MAIN

RHINE

HEALTH SPA *spa town*

BADEN-BADEN

Baden-Württemberg

FERRY

MARTIN LUTHER *religious reformer*

Rheinland-Palatinate

STOLZENFELS CASTLE

CONSTANTINE BASILICA

The custom of decorating CHRISTMAS TREES comes from Germany.

THE CUCKOO CLOCK was invented in the Black Forest mountains.

BLACK FOREST

PORTA NIGRA *city gate*

TRIER

Saar

SAARBRÜCKEN

ALBRECHT DÜRER *painter and draftsman*

VOLKSWAGEN BEETLE

LUCAS

LEONIE

21

- ★ CAPITAL: BERLIN
- 🗣 LANGUAGE: GERMAN
- 👥 POPULATION: 82 MILLION
- 🗺 AREA: 357,022 KM² / 137,847 SQ. MI.

0   25   50   75   100 kilometers
0   25   50 miles

SWITZERLAND

CAPITAL: BERN

LANGUAGES: GERMAN, FRENCH, ITALIAN, ROMANSH

POPULATION: 8 MILLION

AREA: 41,277 KM² / 15,937 SQ. MI.

Schweiz
the country's name in German

Suisse
the country's name in French

Svizzera
the country's name in Italian

Svizra
the country's name in Romansh

JONAS

ANAÏS

Switzerland is famous for producing reliable WATCHES and nifty POCKETKNIVES.

SOLID SWISS BANKS

SAINT BERNARD

city gate SPALEN

PAUL KLEE painter

Basel-Stadt

BASEL

Basel-Landschaft

RHINE

ROMAN THEATER AT AUGUSTA RAURICA

CASTLE

AARAU

Jura

Solothurn

Aargau

Lucern

Aare

① THE HEIDI WEBER MUSEUM displays the work of Le Corbusier.

LE CORBUSIER architect

VACHERIN CHEESE

COW

WINE

CASTLE

LAKE BIEL

NEUCHÂTEL

CATHEDRAL

ZYTGLOGGE clock tower

SUGAR BEETS

WHEAT

Neuchâtel

Lake Neuchâtel

LAKE MURTEN

BERN

AARE

Bern

POTATOES

ZÄHRINGEN BRIDGE

FRIBOURG

Fribourg

CATTLE FARMING

MILK

LAKE THUN

LAKE BRIENZ

③

JUNGFRAU

MÖNCH

EIGER ④

BERNESE ALPS

Vaud

GRAPEVINES

CATHEDRAL

LAUSANNE ②

CHÂTEAU DE CHILLON

CHÂTEAU DE TOURBILLON

VALÈRE BASILICA

RHÔNE

DUFOURSPITZE
4,634 meters / 15,203 ft.
Switzerland's highest peak

LAKE GENEVA

THE JET D'EAU,
the highest fountain in Europe,
jetting water up to a height
of 140 meters / 460 feet

RHÔNE

GENEVA

Geneva

SION

Valais

MATTERHORN
4,478 meters / 14,692 ft.

SCIENTISTS AT THE CERN RESEARCH CENTER
This huge laboratory is situated near Geneva.

APPLES

② VINEYARDS

THE RED CROSS
is an organization that helps victims of war.

③ SPHINX OBSERVATORY
on the Jungfrau

④ a dangerous climb up the NORTH FACE OF THE EIGER

EDWARD WHYMPER
In 1865 he led an expedition that was the first to conquer the Matterhorn.

PENNINE ALPS

ALPINE ASTERS

22

CERVELAT SAUSAGE

THE RHINE FALLS

Schaffhausen

RHINE

RACLETTE
hard cheese, heated, the melted part is scraped off and eaten

CHOCOLATE

MUESLI
was invented in Switzerland.

SCHWINGEN
Swiss wrestling

Thurgau

LAKE CONSTANCE

EMMENTAL CHEESE

FONDUE
melted hard cheese mixed with wine

FRAUENFELD

WINTERTHUR

THE GROSSMÜNSTER CHURCH

ABBEY OF ST. GALL

Appenzell Ausserrhoden

ST. GALLEN

The abbey library contains valuable BOOKS dating back many centuries.

RÖSTI
a pancake made of thickly grated potato

ZÜRICH

Zürich

HERISAU

APPENZELLER
sheepdog

Appenzell Innerrhoden

APPENZELL

St. Gallen

APPENZELLER CHEESE

HEIDI, the heroine of Johanna Spyri's novel.

A SWISS MAN IN TRADITIONAL GRAUBÜNDEN COSTUME

KAPELLBRÜCKE
wooden bridge

LAKE ZÜRICH

LAKE ZUG

ZUG
Zug

TOWN HALL

THE WALENSEE

MAIENFELD

LANDWASSER VIADUCT

⑤

LUCERNE

SCHWYZ
Schwyz

GLARUS
Glarus

ST. MARTIN'S CHURCH

Nidwalden

LAKE LUCERNE

STANS

ALTDORF

CHUR

Graubünden

SWISS NATIONAL PARK

SARNEN

Obwalden

RHINE

RHAETIAN ALPS

INN

SKIING

Uri

GLARUS ALPS

⑤

LEPONTINE ALPS

P

S

SNOWBOARDING

GROUND SQUIRREL

ALETSCHGLETSCHER
the biggest Alpine glacier

TICINO

Ticino

CASTELGRANDE

SWISS PINE SPRIG

SWISS PINE

ALPINE IBEX

BELLINZONA

SNOW GENTIAN

BLACK SALAMANDER

HIKING THE VIA ALPINA

LAKE MAGGIORE

LUGANO

SCULPTURE by Giacometti, "The Walking Man"

ALBERTO GIACOMETTI
sculptor

PLAYING THE ALPENHORN

EDELWEISS

LAKE LUGANO

WILLIAM TELL
legendary Swiss hero

ALPINE CHOUGH

OTTER

EAGLE-OWL

LINZERTORTE

THE VENUS OF WILLENDORF, a stone figurine sculpted over 20,000 years ago.

⑦

FIR

OAK

THAYATAL NATIONAL PARK

VIENNESE WALTZ

AT A VIENNESE CAFÉ

BLACK STORK

BOHEMIAN FOREST

GMÜND

Lower Austria

CITY GATE

RYE

SUGAR BEETS

GRAPEVINES

WINE

NEW CATHEDRAL

LENTOS ART MUSEUM

WHEAT

KREMS

ST. STEPHEN'S CATHEDRAL

BURGTHEATER, meaning the Castle Theater

POTATOES

LINZ

DANUBE

⑦ TOWN HALL

Upper Austria

WELS

THE BUMMERLHAUS

STEYR

BENIDICTINE ABBEY AT MELK

SANKT PÖLTEN

VIENNA WOODS

SCHÖNBRUNN PALACE

VIENNA

① VIENNA

Vienna

BADEN

THE ATTERSEE

THE TRAUNSEE

TRAUN

OATS

ENNS

LIMESTONE ALPS NATIONAL PARK

WIENER NEUSTADT

EISENSTADT

LEITHA

LAKE NEUSIEDL

M E S T O N E   A L P S

THE HACKLHAUS

RAILWAY VIADUCT OVER THE SEMMERING PASS

SCHLOSS ESTERHÁZY

Lipizzaner horses are schooled AT THE SPANISH RIDING SCHOOL IN VIENNA.

LEOBEN

Burgenland

MUR

Styria

CLOCK TOWER

GRAZ

CATTLE FARMING

EDELWEISS

FIRE SALAMANDER

S T E R N   A L P S

BURGRUINE LANDSKRON

Carinthia

BATHING IN A THERMAL LAKE, THE WÖRTHERSEE

BLACK PINE

VIENNESE COFFEE

VILLACH

THE WÖRTHERSEE

KLAGENFURT

LINDWURM FOUNTAIN

TAFELSPITZ

beef cooked with root vegetables

WIENER SCHNITZEL

a breaded veal cutlet

LIMESTONE ALPS

SMOOTH SNAKE

FOREST DORMOUSE

RAVEN

EUROPEAN GREEN LIZARD

SACHERTORTE Viennese confectioner created by FRANZ SACHER

KAISERSCHMARRN

pancake torn to pieces, served with jam

APPLE STRUDEL

GUSTAV KLIMT painter

SIGMUND FREUD psychiatrist

PATIENT ON SIGMUND FREUD'S COUCH

POLAND

BALTIC SEA

TERN

BLACK-HEADED GULL

FISHING BOAT

SALMON

AMBER

MUTE SWAN

HEL LIGHTHOUSE
the oldest wooden pier in Europe

GDYNIA
SOPOT

SOPOT PIER

GDAŃSK

BEACH CHAIR

STAWA MŁYNY
a windmill-shaped navigation beacon for ships entering the port

ŚWINOUJŚCIE

BEACHGOER

Pomerania

Kashubia

GDAŃSK CRANE
The crane was used to load goods onto ships.

GRANARIES
At one time grains, iron, and salt were stored here.

ELBLĄG

MALBORK

CRUSADER CASTLE AT MALBORK

THE EARTH   THE SUN

Long ago, people believed the sun went around the earth. Nicolaus Copernicus was the first man to popularize the theory that the earth went around the sun.

① NICOLAUS COPERNICUS

KASHUBIAN DESIGNS

SHIPYARD

SZCZECIN

WILD BOAR

RED FOX

TUCHOLA FOREST

The Vistula is Poland's longest river.

VISTULA

NICOLAUS COPERNICUS'S HOUSE

① TORUŃ

ODER

CROOKED FOREST

HAY BALES IN A MEADOW

PREHISTORIC SETTLEMENT AT BISKUPIN

BYDGOSZCZ

TORUŃ GINGERBREAD

Kujavia

GORZÓW WIELKOPOLSKI

WARTA

GNIEZNO the first capital of Poland

VISTULA

PŁOCK

② FRÉDÉRIC CHOPIN
composer and pianist

STRAWBERRIES

CURRANTS

Greater Poland

POZNAŃ
TOWN HALL

DELICIOUS APPLES

③ ŁOWICZ COSTUME

ODER

ZIELONA GÓRA

COW IN PASTURE

POTATOES

PRIEST MILL

ŁÓDŹ
historic factories

ŁOWICZ CUTOUT

YEW TREE AT HENRYKÓW LUBAŃSKI
This is the oldest tree in Poland and is nearly 1,300 years old

TOWN HALL

WHITE STORK

WROCŁAW

CENTENNIAL HALL

Lower Silesia

ODER

JASNA GÓRA MONASTERY

CZĘSTOCHOWA

④ THE WARSAW MERMAID

SUDETES

WEATHER STATION ON MT. ŚNIEŻKA

OPOLE

Upper Silesia

OATS

SKIER

CASTLE AT MOSZNA

STEELWORKS

KATOWICE

PAN TWARDOWSKI
Legendary sorcerer who sold his soul to the devil.

MARMOT

HIGHLANDER FROM PODHALE

BLACK COAL MINE

VISTULA

WAWEL DRAGON

CAPITAL: WARSAW

LANGUAGE: POLISH

POPULATION: 38 MILLION

AREA: 312,685 KM²/ 120,728 SQ. MI.

Polska
the country's name in Polish

OSCYPEK smoked cheese made of sheep's milk

CHAMOIS

0 25 50 75 100 kilometers
0   25   50 miles

26

OLD TOWN AREA

FISHING

GREAT BLACK CORMORANT

EUROPEAN HEDGEHOG

VIADUCTS AT STAŃCZYKI

HORNBEAM LEAF

HORNBEAM

EUROPEAN BEAVER

ELK

WOLF

COOT

GRAY HERON

KAYAKER

EUROPEAN OTTER

Warmia

ELBLĄG CANAL

OLSZTYN

Masuria

MASURIAN LAKE DISTRICT

LAKE HAŃCZA
Poland's deepest lake

SUWAŁKI

Poland's coldest region

CRANE

GRUNWALD

YACHT

ŚNIARDWY
Poland's biggest lake

DRAGONFLY

GREBE

ORTHODOX CHURCH OF THE HOLY GHOST

OAK

ACORNS

OAK LEAF

WHITE-BACKED WOODPECKER

PHEASANT

LYNX

RYE

NAREW

BIAŁYSTOK

The Białowieża Forest is a good place for bird-watching.

RED SQUIRREL

RED DEER

PINE

Mazovia

BUG

BIAŁOWIEŻA FOREST
Small areas of ancient forest have survived here.

② In this house Frédéric Chopin was born.

PALACE OF CULTURE AND SCIENCE

EUROPEAN BISON

BADGER

PINECONES

PICKLED GHERKINS

ŻELAZOWA WOLA

③

WARSAW

④

Podlaskie

ROYAL CASTLE

SIGISMUND'S COLUMN

PARLIAMENT

WIEPRZ

MARKET SQUARE

SPRUCE CONE

SPRUCE

PIEROGI
dumplings filled with cheese, meat, or vegetables

BARTEK OAK

RADOM

This is a very old tree, more than 600 years old.

KAZIMIERZ DOLNY

ROYAL CASTLE

LUBLIN

TAWNY OWL

PORK CHOP

According to legend, witches used to gather on Bald Mountain.

WHITE-TAILED EAGLE

BIGOS
a stew made of meat and cabbage

CHICKEN BROTH

KIELCE

BALD MOUNTAIN

WHEAT

TOWN HALL

ZAMOŚĆ

GOŁĄBKI
minced meat mixed with rice or buckwheat and wrapped in a cabbage leaf

Lesser Poland

KRAKÓW BREAD RING

ROYAL CASTLE ON WAWEL HILL

SUGAR BEETS

BASILICA

SAN

BROWN BEAR

POPPIES

RZESZÓW

BEECH

ŻUREK SOUP

ZOSIA

JAŚ

KRAKÓW

NIEDZICA CASTLE

SHEEP

RUSSIAN ORTHODOX CHURCH

Bieszczady National Park is a place for hiking.

CARPATHIANS

ZAKOPANE

BEECH LEAF

WILD CAT

RYSY 2,499 meters / 8,197 ft., Poland's highest peak

BROWN TROUT

AESCULAPIAN SNAKE
the biggest snake found in Poland

27

CZECH REPUBLIC

- CAPITAL: PRAGUE
- LANGUAGE: CZECH
- POPULATION: 10 MILLION
- AREA: 78,867 KM²/ 30,451 SQ. MI.

25 50 kilometers
0 25 miles

Česko
the country's name in Czech

ORE MOUNTAINS

UPPER PALATINE FOREST

BOHEMIAN FOREST

BOHEMIA

BOHEMIAN SWITZERLAND NATIONAL PARK

TOWN HALL

LIBEREC

Bohemian Paradise

KOST CASTLE

JIČÍN

RUMCAJS
the hero of books by Václav Čtvrtek

BROWN COAL

ÚSTÍ NAD LABEM

MARIANSKY BRIDGE

ELBE

SPRING WITH MEDICINAL PROPERTIES

KARLOVY VARY

MILL COLONNADE

ICE HOCKEY

SOCCER

Writer FRANZ KAFKA lived in Prague.

ANTONÍN DVOŘÁK
composer and conductor

ZDENĚK MILER
wrote cartoons about Mole

CATHEDRAL

PLZEŇ BEER

PYGMY SHREW

WHEAT

BICYCLING

BOUBÍNSKÝ FOREST

EARLY MORELS

ČESKÝ FOUSEK

LYNX

CHARLES BRIDGE

PRAGUE OLD TOWN

KARLŠTEJN CASTLE

ST. BARBARA'S CHURCH

KUTNÁ HORA

EUROPEAN ADDER

PARTRIDGE

VLTAVA

POTATOES

HLUBOKÁ CASTLE

CARP

MARKET SQUARE

ČESKÉ BUDĚJOVICE

ČESKÝ KRUMLOV

TŘEBOŇSKO NATURE RESERVE

CASTLE

BROOK LAMPREY

MARSH HARRIER

ANNA TOMÁŠ EUROPEAN MOLE

GREATER MOUSE-EARED BAT

HISTORIC HOUSES
in the village of Holašovice

OTTER

PINE MARTEN

GOLDENEYE

BIRD WATCHING

HARRIER CHICKS

Bohemian Forest National Park

28

GANNET

THE LUMIÈRE BROTHERS were the first filmmakers.

France is a major producer of CARS.

THE CHANNEL TUNNEL runs under the English Channel, linking France and the United Kingdom.

ENGLISH CHANNEL

CLAUDE MONET painted Rouen cathedral.

OLD STOCK EXCHANGE

Nord-Pas de Calais

LILLE

SUGAR BEETS

Picardy

GOTHIC CATHEDRAL

EIFFEL TOWER

SACRÉ-COEUR BASILICA

MONT SAINT-MICHEL

CLIFFS

ROUEN

THE LOUVRE PYRAMID

PARIS

Île-de-France

PHARE DU FOUR LIGHTHOUSE

RUINS OF RICHARD THE LIONHEART'S CASTLE

Normandy

ROCKY COAST

BREST

HISTORIC OLD HOUSES

PALACE OF VERSAILLES ①

Brittany

THE CARNAC STONES

RENNES

Pays de la Loire

RAPESEED

EDIBLE FROG

LOIRE France's longest river

BRETON WOMAN IN TRADITIONAL COSTUME

CHÂTEAU DES DUCS DE BRETAGNE

CHÂTEAU DE CHENONCEAU

FISHING BOAT

NANTES

FUTUROSCOPE theme park featuring the latest technologies

Centre

BOURGES

ATLANTIC OCEAN

SARDINE

Oléron

HARBOR TOWER

LA ROCHELLE

SUNFLOWERS

EDIBLE SNAIL

Auvergne

Poitou-Charentes

LIMOUSIN CATTLE

EXTINCT VOLCANOES

OYSTER BEDS

MASSIF CENTRAL

LOBSTER

Limousin

WINE

ROCK PAINTINGS IN THE CAVES AT LASCAUX

MILLAU VIADUCT 341 meters / 1,119 feet high

LAGUIOLE KNIFE

BAY OF BISCAY

BORDEAUX

LAGUIOLE

ZOÉ

LOUIS

THE GREAT DUNE OF PYLA Europe's biggest sand dune

TRUFFLES

Acquitaine

CORN

GARONNE

THE AIRBUS is built here

Midi-Pyrénées

Languedoc

HIKING in the Pyrenees

PELOTA Basque game

PYRENEAN CHAMOIS

TOULOUSE

CANALS linking the Mediterranean Sea and the Atlantic

BEACH

EDELWEISS

Roussillon

PÉTANQUE a game in which the players throw metal balls toward a smaller, wooden ball

PYRENEAN BROOK SALAMANDER

PYRENEAN DESMAN

PYRENEES

30

France

French writer **CHARLES PERRAULT** wrote the fairy tales "Puss in Boots," "Cinderella," and "Little Red Riding Hood."

PARIS is the world capital of fashion.

MARIANNE, the warrior in a Phrygian cap, is the symbol of liberty and the French state.

The country's name is spelled the same in French as in English.

Many famous **PERFUMES** are made in France.

ROOSTER the emblem of France

0   50   100 kilometers
0   25   50 miles

👑 CAPITAL: PARIS

👅 LANGUAGE: FRENCH

👤👤👤 POPULATION: 66 MILLION

⬚ AREA: 551,500 KM² / 212,935 SQ. MI.

① **THE GARDENS OF VERSAILLES** are in the French style: symmetrical and formally laid out.

LOUIS XIV THE SUN KING

ARDENNES

Ardennes

RED FOX

WHEAT

CHAMPAGNE sparkling wine from Champagne

Lorraine

Champagne

SEINE

GRAPEVINES

PORTE GUILLAUME

famous **DIJON MUSTARD**

DIJON

Burgundy

VOSGES

Alsace

CATHEDRAL

PONTS COUVERTS

STRASBOURG

WHITE STORK

BAGUETTES

CROISSANT a French pastry

FROGS' LEGS

RATATOUILLE a dish of stewed vegetables

SNAILS

DESCARTES brilliant philosopher and mathematician

Jura Franche-Comté

TGV high-speed railway

NOTRE-DAME DE FOURVIÈRE BASILICA

LAKE GENEVA

CRÊPES are popular all over France.

CAMEMBERT

ROQUEFORT

France is famous for its delicious cheeses.

MAGPIE

BADGER

BRIE

BANON cheese wrapped in chestnut leaves

MONT BLANC 4,810 meters / 15,771 ft., Europe's highest peak

THE ALPS attract skiers.

CHAMONIX

LYON

RHÔNE

Rhône-Alpes

GRENOBLE

SWEET CHESTNUT LEAVES

SWEET CHESTNUTS

EUROPEAN HEDGEHOG

PONT-DU-GARD AQUEDUCT

FLAMINGOES can be seen in the Rhône delta.

②

LAVENDER fields bloom in Provence.

③

TOUR DE FRANCE The competitors in this bike race have to ride 3,000 kilometers / 1,800 miles.

NAPOLEON'S HAT

NAPOLEON was a military commander and emperor of France in the 19th century.

ROMAN PHITHEATER

PAPAL PALACE

AVIGNON

NÎMES

③

Provence

NICE

ARLES

②

CANNES

MARSEILLE TOULON

Côte d'Azur

GOLFE DU LION

CHÂTEAU D'IF

FILM FESTIVAL

YACHT

MEDITERRANEAN SEA

Corsica

BASTIA

Corsica

AJACCIO

FILITOSA stone-carved warriors

MEDITERRANEAN SEA

PASSENGER FERRY

31

THE TOWER OF HERCULES
the world's oldest working lighthouse

DOLMEN AT AXEITOS
a prehistoric tomb

COD

FISHING PORT

Galicia

CATHEDRAL

• SANTIAGO DE COMPOSTELA

• VIGO

CATTLE FARMING

HOOPOE

CHURCH OF ST. MICHAEL OF LILLO

Asturias

• OVIEDO

Cantabria

SANTANDER

GUGGENHEIM MUSEUM

BILBAO

Basqu

CORDILLERA CANTÁBRICA

• LEÓN

CAVE OF ALTAMIRA
prehistoric paintings

BURGOS

Castilla y León

OLIVE OIL
is a Spanish specialty

IBERIAN WOLF

FIGS

FIG

DON QUIXOTE AND SANCHO PANZA
the heroes of Miguel Cervantes's novel

• VALLADOLID

ROMAN AQUEDUCT

ALCAZAR

Spain's oldest UNIVERSITY

SALAMANCA

FORTIFICATIONS

• SEGOVIA

THE PR.. MUSEUM

TAPAS
small dishes

ALMONDS

ÁVILA •

PUERTA DE EUROPA TOWERS

SISTEMA CENTRAL

BLACK STORK

Madrid

MADRID •

GAZPACHO
a cold soup made of tomatoes, cucumbers, and peppers with bread and olive oil

ALMOND

SPANISH TORTILLA
made with eggs and potatoes

STATUE OF A BEAR AT THE PUERTA DEL SOL

TAGUS

ALCAZAR

• TOLEDO

SANGRÍA
an iced punch with a wine base to which fruit, sugar, and brandy or seltzer are added

PAELLA
a dish of rice and saffron with seafood or meat and vegetables

Estremadura

ROMAN AMPHITHEATER

SHEEP FARMING

Castilla

WHEAT

WINDMILL

• MÉRIDA

FAMOUS SPANISH PAINTERS

DIEGO VELÁZQUEZ

FRANCISCO GOYA

PABLO PICASSO

SALVADOR DALÍ

BLACK IBERIAN PIGS

BUSTARD

MEZQUITA
Great Mosque

CATHEDRAL

Andalucía

SPANISH GUITAR

TORRE DEL ORO

SEVILLE

CORK OAK

GUADALQUIVIR

• CÓRDOBA

WINE CORKS

THE ALHAMBRA
fortified palace of the caliphs

GRANADA

CORRIDA
bullfighting

IBERIAN LYNX

CARS
are produced in Spain.

FLAMENCO DANCER

CATHEDRAL

ARENA

• CÁDIZ
is the oldest city in Spain.

MÁLAGA

SIERRA NEVADA

GIBRALTAR
(United Kingdom)

ATLANTIC OCEAN

STRAIT OF GIBRALTAR

SPAIN

BROWN BEAR

THE OSBORNE BULL

SOCCER is a popular sport in Spain.

The roadside silhouette of a bull is the emblem of Spain.

España — the country's name in Spanish

CAPITAL: MADRID

LANGUAGES: SPANISH (CASTILIAN) as well as Catalan, Galician, and Basque

POPULATION: 47 MILLION

AREA: 505,370 KM²/ 195,124 SQ. MI.

kilometers
0 25 50 100
0 25 50 miles

wine country

WINE

Navarra

PAMPLONA

LOGROÑO

la Rioja

GRAPEVINES

Aragón

PYRENEES

Catalonia

ALJAFERÍA PALACE

ZARAGOZA

EBRO

SANTA MARIA DE MONTSERRAT MONASTERY

SAGRADA FAMÍLIA CHURCH

BARCELONA

PAULA

DANIEL

4

BUILDING TOWERS OF PEOPLE is a traditional Catalan entertainment.

La Mancha

Sistema Ibérico

HANGING HOUSES

STRAWBERRIES

TARRAGONA

RUINS OF A ROMAN AMPHITHEATER

MEDITERRANEAN DWARF PALM

CUENCA

RELAXING ON THE BEACH

GOLFO DE VALENCIA

Balearic Islands

ENSAÏMADA traditional pastry

MANCHEGO sheep's milk cheese

CITY OF ARTS AND SCIENCES

Mallorca

PALMA

Minorca

SAFFRON

Valencia

VALENCIA

MUSSELS

Ibiza

YACHT

Cabrera

SEASIDE VACATIONS

ORANGES

CASTLE OF SANTA BÁRBARA

Formentera

CATHEDRAL

MURCIA

Murcia

ALICANTE

CANARY

HOBARA BUSTARD

MEDITERRANEAN SEA

EGYPTIAN VULTURE

SURFING

OLIVE TREE

GREEN AND BLACK OLIVES

Canary Islands

CANARY ISLAND DATE PALM

WINDMILL

Lanzarote

MULHACÉN 3,478 meters / 11,407 ft., Spain's highest peak

TEIDE VOLCANO 3,718 meters / 12,198 ft

BANANA TREE

La Palma

CRAYFISH

SANTA CRUZ DE TENERIFE

Fuerteventura

Gomera

Tenerife

LAS PALMAS DE GRAN CANARIA

Gran Canaria

Hierro

ATLANTIC OCEAN

33

BARI

Apulia

CASTELLO SVEVO

VIA APPIA ancient Roman road

SHEEP

Basilicata

Calabria

IONIAN SEA.

ROSEMARY

ORANGES

RED MULLET

BAY TREE

Campania

VESUVIUS volcano

POMPEII the ruins of a city destroyed by an eruption of Vesuvius

BAY LEAVES are used as a seasoning.

JULIUS CAESAR ruler and politician in ancient Rome

ANNULAR SEA BREAM

CATANIA

SYRACUSE

MONASTERY AT MONTE CASSINO

NAPLES

CASTEL DELL'OVO

BOAT

CHURCH OF SAN CATALDO

PALERMO

ETNA volcano

Sicily

LEMONS

GRAPEVINES

AGRIGENTO

Sicily is the biggest island in the Mediterranean Sea.

COMMON TORPEDO

TYRRHENIAN SEA

ANCIENT GREEK TEMPLE

MEDITERRANEAN SEA

kilometers
0   50   100
0 25 50 miles

EUROPEAN HAKE

The story of ROMEO AND JULIET (the heroes of William Shakespeare's play) is set in Verona.

MARCO POLO a famous traveler who reached China in medieval times

NURAGHE ancient tower

RELAXING ON THE BEACH

Sardinia

CAGLIARI

Sardinia

MOZZARELLA CHEESE

PINOCCHIO hero of the book by Carlo Collodi

ITALIA the country's name in Italian

OLIVES

MOUFLON

FRANCESCA

RICCARDO

Italy

🏛 CAPITAL: ROME

🍴 LANGUAGE: ITALIAN

⚓ POPULATION: 61 MILLION

AREA: 301,340 KM²/ 116,348 SQ. MI.

35

BROWN BEAR

IVAN MEŠTROVIĆ
sculptor

BEECH

LONG-FINGERED
BAT

TRUFFLES

LYNX

HAZEL GROUSE

IRIS CROATICA

Grows only in Croatia

TRAKOŠĆAN
CASTLE

MUR

VARAŽDIN

CATHEDRAL

Central Croatia

RISNJAK
NATIONAL PARK

HAZEL DORMOUSE

VIEW OF THE
OLD TOWN
FROM ABOVE

ZAGREB

CLOCK
TOWER

OYSTER FARMING

VIEW OF THE
EUPHRASIAN
BASILICA

FORTRESS

KARLOVAC

KUPA

SISAK

OYSTERS

POREČ

RIJEKA

Gorski Kotar

CORN

Croatia
includes more than
one thousand
ISLANDS

Istria

ROMAN
AMPHITHEATER

PULA

Krk

Pag

UNA

PLITVIČKA
LAKES
NATIONAL
PARK

PARASAILING

LIGHTHOUSE
on the island of Porer

Cres

Rab

Lošinj

Lika

D
I
N
A
R
I
C

VELEBIT

ALKA

CHEESE
FROM PAG
ISLAND

Premuda

Unije

Olib

Molat

DINARA
1,830 meters / 6,004
Croatia's
highest peak

SINJSKA ALKA
a traditional equestrian
tournament held in
the town of Sinj

SUNBATHING

CHURCH OF THE
HOLY CROSS

NIN

ZADAR
①

CATHEDRAL
OF ST. JAMES

KRKA

VRLIKA

ADRIATIC
SEA

SAILING

Dugi Otok

Pašman

A
L
M
A
T
I
A

MOREŠKA
a sword dance
performed
in Korčula

Ugljan

SINJ
③

BLUE
GROTTO

DIVING

ŠIBENIK

Kornat

Žirje

TROGIR
②

SPLIT

on the island of Biševo

THE TOWN OF KORČULA

Čiovo

Šolta

KITE SURFING

HVAR

Svetac

Vis

on the island of Korčula

Biševo

Suša

BENEDICTINE MONASTERY

PICIGIN
a game played with a small ball in shallow water

on the island of Mljet

CASTLE

PINE MARTEN

ORNAMENTS
decorating old
Croatian churches

OLIVE OIL

BRUDET
fish stew

ORAHNJAČA
a nut roll

LICITARSKO SRCE
gingerbread heart,
a traditional gift

OAK

FIRS

GREAT EGRET

PRŠUT
cured ham

BLACK RISOTTO
colored with squid ink

ŠTRUKLI
pastry with cheese

JELOVAR

DRAVA

Slavonia

PRUSSIAN CARP

CITRUS FRUITS

KULEN
spicy sausage with paprika

SUGAR BEETS

PAPUK GEOPARK

MARKET SQUARE

KOPAČKI RIT NATURE PARK

CATHEDRAL

OSIJEK

SAVA

POŽEGA

WHEAT

ĐAKOVO

DANUBE

COOT

EUROPEAN SHAG

SLAVONSKI BROD

VINKOVCI

SAVA

PIKE

HAT FROM THE LIKA REGION

OLM

TRADITIONAL COSTUME FROM VRLIKA

WHITE-THROATED DIPPER

GRAY WAGTAIL

GRAYLAG GOOSE

BUNJA
stone houses built in ancient Croatia

CHURCH OF ST. DONATUS

TRADITIONAL FOLK COSTUME

KOLO FOLK DANCE

HAT FROM ŠIBENIK

THE TIE
has its origins in neckerchiefs worn by Croatians in days of old.

KRKA NATIONAL PARK

KAMERLENGO CASTLE
②

BUR CLOVER

ORANGE TREE

GUSLE
a traditional stringed instrument

CROATIAN BAGPIPES

DIOCLETIAN'S PALACE
③

MOUNTAIN CICADA

DALMATIAN

OLIVE GROVES

LAVENDER

FIGS

PETRA

LUKA

OLIVES

FIG TREE

GRAPEVINES

OLD TOWN SURROUNDED BY STONE WALLS

0   50 kilometers
0   25 miles

Hvar

Korčula

KORČULA

Mljet

ONOFRIO'S FOUNTAIN

DUBROVNIK

Croatia

CAPITAL: ZAGREB

LANGUAGE: CROATIAN

Hrvatska
the country's name in Croatian

POPULATION: 4 MILLION

AREA: 56,594 KM²/ 21,851 SQ. MI.

37

Romania

- 👑 CAPITAL: BUCHAREST
- 👅 LANGUAGE: ROMANIAN
- 👨‍👩‍👧 POPULATION: 19 MILLION
- ↗ AREA: 238,391 KM² / 92,000 SQ. MI.

0 — 25 — 50 kilometers
0 — 25 miles

WOODEN CHURCHES in the Maramureș region

ROMÂNIA
↑
the country's name in Romanian

TRADITIONAL COSTUMES from the Maramureș region

Maramureș

colorful tombstones at the MERRY CEMETERY

GREATER NOCTULE BAT

A large number of cave-bear skeletons were found in the Bear Cave.

BEAR CAVE

BARBASTELLE

ANDREI   IOANA

CAVE BEARS lived thousands of years ago.

ORADEA

Crișana

ST. MICHAEL'S CHURCH

CLUJ-NAPOCA

Transylvania

CLOCK TOWER

COUNT DRACULA was a vampire, the hero of Bram Stoker's book. Dracula lived in a castle in Transylvania. ①

APUSENI MOUNTAINS

TOWN HALL

TRADITIONAL COSTUMES from the Sibiu region

SIGHIȘOARA

ARAD

MUREȘ

HUNYADI CASTLE

MOLDOVEANU 2,544 meters / 8,317 ft., Romania's highest peak

Banat

CHURCH

TIMIȘOARA

"BIRD IN SPACE," a sculpture by Constantin Brâncuși

sculptor CONSTANTIN BRÂNCUȘI   ruins of FORTRESSES built by the ancient Dacians ②

TISMANA MONASTERY

TRANSYLVANIAN ALPS

②

"ENDLESS COLUMN," a sculpture by Constantin Brâncuși

SPHINX IN THE BUCEGI MOUNTAINS

WINE

TÂRGU JIU

NICOLAE ROMANESCU PARK

OLT

MITITEI grilled sausages with garlic

STATUE OF DECEBALUS a 40-meter / 130-foot-high rock sculpture, the biggest in Europe

THE IRON GATES a rocky gorge through which the Danube flows

CRAIOVA

CORN

CIORBĂ a kind of sour soup

ARDEI UMPLUȚI stuffed peppers

DAM

BARLEY

POTATOES

SARMALE

a filling made of meat and rice wrapped in cabbage or vine leaves

MĂMĂLIGĂ porridge made from yellow corn flour

OINĂ a traditional Romanian sport similar to baseball

SKIER

DANUBE

HEDGEHOG

SUCEVIȚA FORTIFIED MONASTERY

Bukovina

BLACK GROUSE

BEECH

OAK

RED FOX

BROWN BEAR

PAINTED CHURCHES

PAINTED EGGS

WILD BOAR

EASTERN CARPATHIANS

PALACE OF CULTURE

RACCOON DOG

LYNX

WOLF

IAȘI

HIKING

EUROPEAN POLECAT

QUAIL

VÂNĂTORI-NEAMȚ NATURAL PARK

Moldavia

PRUT

CAMPING

MEADOW VIPER

PLUMS

BACĂU

SIRET

RYE

GREAT EGRET

BEE-EATER

FALLOW DEER

GRAPEVINES

CHURCH

EUROPEAN ROLLER

BLACK-WINGED STILT

SPOONBILL

OLD TOWN

BIRD-WATCHING

DALMATIAN PELICAN

BRAȘOV

BLACK CHURCH

GALAȚI

PELEȘ CASTLE

BRĂILA

CRUISES ON THE DANUBE

HUCHEN

DANUBE DELTA

SUNBATHING ON THE BEACH

BRAN CASTLE is known as Dracula's castle ①

achia

Dobruja

PLOIEȘTI

PALACE OF THE PARLIAMENT

SUGAR BEETS

HISTORIC CASINO

SEA ANEMONE

TRIUMPHAL ARCH

SHIPYARD

BUCHAREST

CARP

CONSTANȚA

WHEAT

HORSE MACKEREL

DANUBE

ROMANIAN HAMSTER

MUSKRAT

FISHING

BEACH

BLACK SEA

39

BANK VOLE

EUROPEAN CAT SNAKE

JUDAS TREE

GROUND SQUIRREL

RHODOPES

THYME

JUDAS-TREE BLOSSOM

DOJRAN LAKE

LAKE PRESPA

Thrace

BROWN BEAR

Macedonia

STRUMA

TOBACCO COTTON

BARLEY

WHITE TOWER

VIKOS GORGE

ALIÁKMON

● THESSALONIKI

Thasos

Samothrace

Epirus

OLYMPUS
2,917 meters / 9,570 ft.
Greece's highest mountain range

GREATER PIPEFISH

Lemnos

GOAT FARMING

P I N D U S

MONASTERY at Metéora

● LARISSA

Agios Efstratios

Corfu

● VOLOS

Skiathos

Skyros

I o n i a n   I s l a n d s

SHEEP FARMING

WHEAT

CORN

Skopelos Alónnisos

AEGEAN SEA

Thessaly

IONIAN SEA

Central Greece

Euboea

A
e
g
e
a
n

Psará

Cephalonia

Ithaca

ROMAN ODEON

THE RUINS AT DELPHI

THE PARTHENON

Leukás

CYPRESS

Attica

PIRAEUS

Andros

WINDMILL

BOTTLENOSE DOLPHIN

Zakynthos

● PATRAS

① TREASURY OF ATREUS
a tomb

● ATHENS

Salamis

Kéa

Tinos

OLYMPIA

② MYCENAE ③

Aegina

Kythnos

Syros

Mykonos

TEMPLE OF APOLLO

Peloponnese

Serifos

Paros

Naxos

LOGGERHEAD SEA TURTLE

BEACH

THE RUINS OF ANCIENT SPARTA

Peloponnese peninsula

Sifnos

C
y
c
l
a
d
e
s

YACHT

Melos

Folegandros

Ios

ARCHITECTURE
on the island of Santorini

Sikinos

Santorini

WATER-SKIING

Kythira

LIGHTHOUSE

SEA OF CRETE

ROCCA AL MARE FORTRESS

MEDITERRANEAN MONK SEAL

● CHANIA

● HERAKLION

MEDITERRANEAN SEA

Crete

Crete

PALACE AT KNOSSOS

GREECE

FETA CHEESE

PITA BREAD

TOMATOES

BASIL

EVROS

OLIVE OIL

OLIVES

EGGPLANT

GREEK SALAD

CAPITAL: ATHENS Ελλάδα

← the country's name in Greek

LANGUAGE: GREEK

POPULATION: 11 MILLION

AREA: 131,957 KM²/ 50,949 SQ. MI.

DILL

WINE

OREGANO

FASOLADA
bean soup

TZATZIKI
an appetizer made with yogurt, cucumber, garlic, and olive oil

GYRO
meat roasted on a spit, wrapped in pita bread, and served with fries and tomatoes

ANEMONES

0   25   50   100 kilometers / 50 miles

MOUSSAKA
a dish made of eggplant and minced meat

OLIVE TREE

SOUVLAKI
meat grilled on a skewer with vegetables

DIMITRA

NIKOLAOS

In Greek mythology, THE SIRENS were half woman, half bird.

GREEK ROCK LIZARD

ANCIENT GREEKS

PYTHAGORAS
mathematician and philosopher

In Greek mythology, THE CENTAURS were half man, half horse.

GRAPEVINES

Lesbos

A GREEK IN TRADITIONAL COSTUME

ALMOND TREE

ALMONDS

COMMON CHAMELEON

GOLDEN JACKAL

Chios

RUINS OF THE TEMPLE OF HERA

GREEN TOAD

NIGHTINGALE

ARCHAEOLOGISTS research the remains of ancient civilizations.

$a^2 + b^2 = c^2$

PYTHAGORAS'S THEOREM

HOMER
poet

Ikaria   Samos

GREAT WHITE PELICAN

HERMANN'S TORTOISE

BOY PLAYING AN AULOS

LYRE

③ ANCIENT THEATER AT EPIDAURUS

Patmos   Leipsoi

Leros   Kalymnos

Amorgos   Kos

Nisyros

PALACE OF THE GRAND MASTER OF THE KNIGHTS OF RHODES

ANCIENT GREEK VASES

The first OLYMPIC GAMES were held in ancient Greece, at the town of Olympia. ①

Astypalaia   Tilos

Simi

Kalkis   Rhodes

RHODES

Kastelorizo

In ancient Greece, there were many brilliant PHILOSOPHERS.

Karpathos

SOCRATES

PLATO

ARISTOTLE

THE MASK OF AGAMEMNON found in an ancient grave at Mycenae ②

Kasos

Dodecanese Islands

TRADITIONAL GREEK SHIP

MEDITERRANEAN SEA

41

ASIA

49 COUNTRIES

POPULATION: 4 BILLION 223 MILLION

AREA: 44,391,162 KM² / 17,139,445 SQ. MI.

0 250 500 750 1000 kilometers
0 250 500 miles

KARA SEA

MOSCOW

BLACK SEA

ASTANA

KAZAKHSTAN

GEORGIA
TBILISI

ARMENIA
YEREVAN

AZERBAIJAN
BAKU

CASPIAN SEA

UZBEKISTAN
TASHKENT

KYRGYZSTAN
BISHKEK

ANKARA

TURKEY

NICOSIA
CYPRUS

SYRIA
DAMASCUS

LEBANON
BEIRUT

ISRAEL

JERUSALEM

AMMAN
JORDAN

BAGHDAD
IRAQ

KUWAIT CITY

KUWAIT

TEHRAN

TURKMENISTAN
ASHGABAT

IRAN

TAJIKISTAN
DUSHANBE

AFGHANISTAN
KABUL

BAHRAIN
MANAMA

ISLAMABAD

RIYADH

SAUDI
ARABIA

DOHA
QATAR

ABU DHABI

UNITED
ARAB
EMIRATES

MUSCAT

OMAN

PAKISTAN

SANA

YEMEN

ARABIAN
SEA

OLIVE RIDLEY
SEA TURTLE

RED SEA

DOLPHIN

INDIA

42

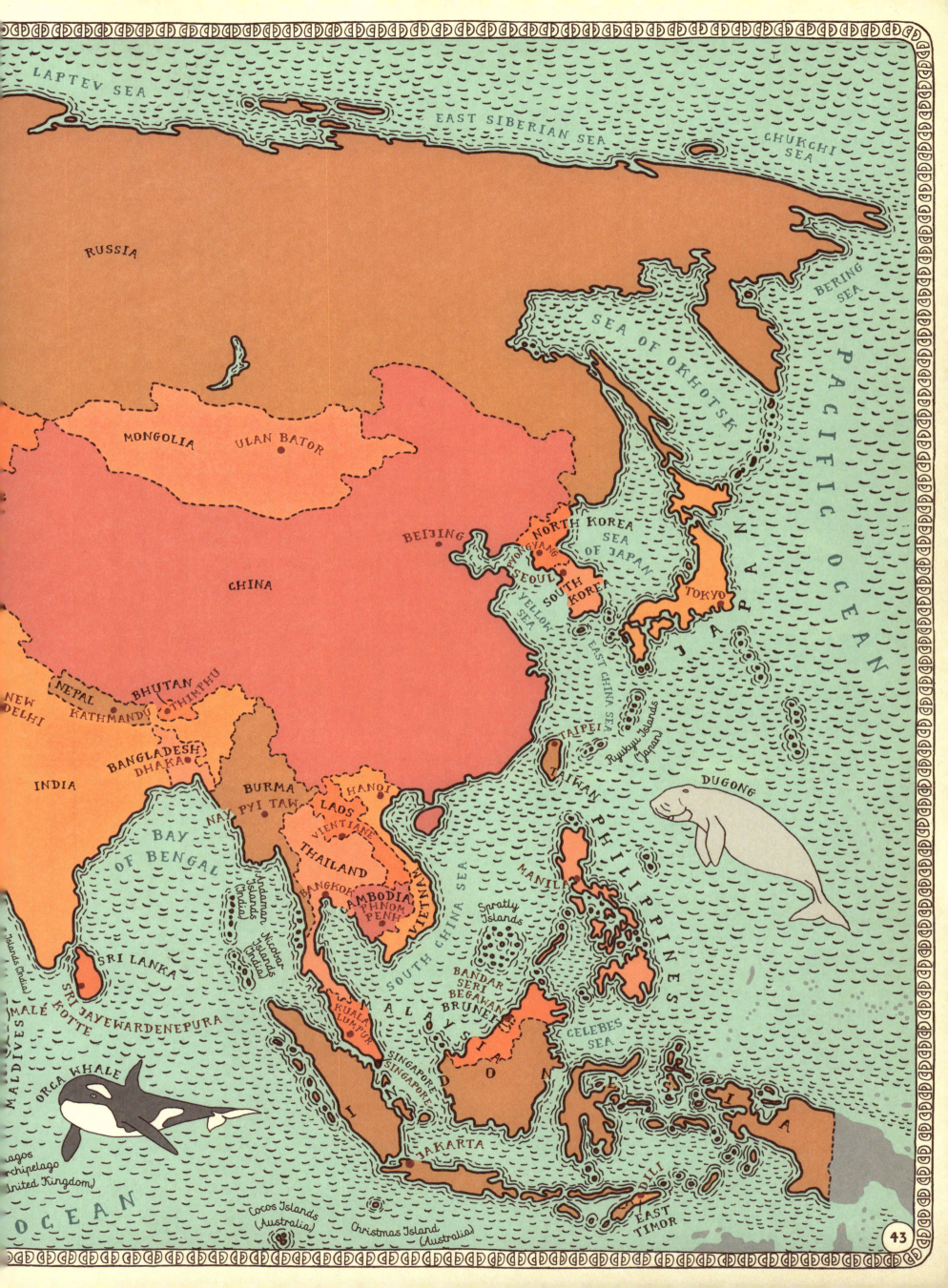

LAPTEV SEA

EAST SIBERIAN SEA

CHUKCHI SEA

RUSSIA

BERING SEA

MONGOLIA

ULAN BATOR

SEA OF OKHOTSK

PACIFIC OCEAN

BEIJING

NORTH KOREA

SEA OF JAPAN

PYONGYANG

SEOUL

SOUTH KOREA

TOKYO

CHINA

YELLOW SEA

J A P A N

EAST CHINA SEA

TAIPEI

NEPAL

BHUTAN

Ryukyu Islands (Japan)

NEW DELHI

KATHMANDU

THIMPHU

TAIWAN

DUGONG

BANGLADESH

DHAKA

BURMA

HANOI

INDIA

NAY PYI TAW

LAOS

VIENTIANE

PHILIPPINES

BAY OF BENGAL

THAILAND

Andaman Islands (India)

BANGKOK

CAMBODIA

PHNOM PENH

MANILA

SPRATLY Islands

SRI LANKA

Nicobar Islands (India)

SOUTH CHINA SEA

BANDAR SERI BEGAWAN

BRUNEI

CELEBES SEA

MALDIVES

MALÉ

KUALA LUMPUR

SRI JAYEWARDENEPURA KOTTE

SINGAPORE

SINGAPORE

MALAYSIA

ORCA WHALE

I N D O N E S I A

...gos Archipelago (United Kingdom)

JAKARTA

DILI

EAST TIMOR

O C E A N

Cocos Islands (Australia)

Christmas Island (Australia)

Russia

РОССИЯ
← the country's name written in Russian

👑 CAPITAL: MOSCOW

👅 LANGUAGES: RUSSIAN and many others used in various parts of the country

👤👤👤 POPULATION: 142 MILLION

AREA: 17,098,242 KM²/ 6,601,668 SQ. MI.

Russia is the largest country in the world.

0   250   500 kilometers
0   250 miles

BROWN BEAR

PYOTR TCHAIKOVSKY composed the music for the famous ballets "The Nutcracker" and "Swan Lake."

DMITRI MENDELEEV chemist

BALLET

Franz Josef Land

Severnaya Zemlya

Novaya Zemlya

KARA SEA

ELENA

VLADIMIR

WOODEN CHURCHES on the island of Kizhi on Lake Onega

PORT

NATURAL GAS EXTRACTION

BALTIC SEA

KING'S GATE

KALININGRAD

THE HERMITAGE art gallery is in the WINTER PALACE.

LAKE LADOGA

ST. PETERSBURG

MURMANSK

BARENTS SEA

FABERGÉ EGG The work of the tsar's jeweler with a miniature carriage inside it

LAKE ONEGA

ARCHANGELSK

TRADITIONAL NENETS TENT made from reindeer skins

URALS

YENISEY

SWIMMING

BEACHES

ST. BASIL'S CATHEDRAL

NIZHNY NOVGOROD KREMLIN

EUROPE ASIA

KUL SHARIF MOSQUE IN KAZAN

OB

BIRCH

S I

MOSQUITO

MOSCOW VLADIMIR

ST. DEMETRIUS'S CATHEDRAL

NIZHNY NOVGOROD

SUNFLOWERS

KAZAN KREMLIN

KAZAN

PERM

YEKATE-RINBURG

CRUDE OIL EXTRACTION

ST. NIKOLAI'S CHAPEL

ROSTOV-ON-DON

VOLGOGRAD

VOLGA

SAMARA

UFA

CHELY-ABINSK

OMSK

NOVOSIBIRSK

SOCHI

ELBRUS 5,612 meters / 18,510 ft., Russia's highest peak

EUROPEAN HAMSTER

CORN

WHEAT

VALENKI felt boots

USHANKA HAT WITH EAR FLAPS

BARLEY

BLACK SEA

CAUCASUS

CASPIAN SEA

SAMOVAR

ELK

ALTAI

BELUKHA 4,506 meters / 14,783 ft.

MATRYOSHKA DOLL

COULIBIAC a large pasty stuffed with fish, rice, and vegetables

BEEF STROGANOFF sirloin steak fried with mushrooms and onion, with tomatoes and cream added

PELMENI meat dumplings

GOOSEBERRIES

BLACKCURRANTS

CAVIAR canapés

BLINIS pancakes made with yeast

ICONS BY ANDREI RUBLEV

44

ICEBREAKER

ARCTIC OCEAN

ICEBOUND OCEAN

EAST SIBERIAN SEA

Wrangel Island

New Siberian Islands

POLAR BEAR

SPECTACLED EIDER

SIBERIAN HUSKY

THE CHUKCHI
an indigenous people

BERING SEA

GYRFALCON

LAPTEV SEA

ARCTIC FOX

KOLYMA

Kamchatka

VOLCANOES

THE NENETS
an indigenous people
who inhabit Siberia

TUNDRA

REINDEER

Mammoths died out more
than 10,000 years ago.

YAKUTSKY OSTROG TOWER

SEVERE FROSTS
-70°C

MAGADAN

SEA OF OKHOTSK

DIAMONDS

LENA

MAMMOTH R

CRESTED AUKLET

POLLOCK

TAIGA

LENA PILLARS
picturesque rocks

YAKUTSK

MAMMOTH REMAINS
can be seen
in a museum in Yakutsk.

BLACK COAL

LARCH CONE

SIBERIAN LARCH

BOHEMIAN WAXWING

THE TRANS-SIBERIAN RAILROAD
is the world's longest railroad line
(almost 9,200 kilometers / 5,780 miles long).
It runs from Moscow to Vladivostok.

route of the
Trans-Siberian
Railroad

Sakhalin

B E

TRADITIONAL WOODEN ARCHITECTURE

GREAT TIT

the world's
deepest
lake,
1,620 meters /
5,315 ft.
deep

RUSSIAN RATSNAKE

SIBERIAN TIGER

METEORITE

S-56 SUBMARINE

KRASNOYARSK

SAYANS

LAKE BAIKAL

IRKUTSK

BAIKAL SEAL

ORIENTAL FIRE-BELLIED TOAD

VLADIVOSTOK

SEA OF JAPAN

SPUTNIK 1
was the first
satellite put
into Earth's orbit
by man

CCCP

YURI GAGARIN
was the first man
in space

TRADITIONAL COSTUMES

SIBERIAN IBEX

BALALAIKA

SPARROWHAWK

WASSILY KANDINSKY
painter

NIKOLAI GOGOL
writer

ALEXANDER PUSHKIN
poet

45

A MONGOL PLAYING A MORIN KHUUR

WINGED HORSE from the emblem of Mongolia

MORIN KHUUR an instrument with two strings made of horsehair.

ARCHERY ON HORSEBACK

PALLAS'S CAT

SABLE

TAIGA

The Dukha people are REINDEER herders.

DUKHAN TEPEE

HUNTING WITH AN EAGLE

NAYRAMADLIN 4,374 meters / 14,354 ft., Mongolia's highest peak

ULAANGOM

UVS LAKE Mongolia's biggest lake

DELGERMÖRÖN

LAKE HÖVSGÖL

COPPER MINE

RELICT GULL

DEER STONES prehistoric carved megaliths

IDER

ERDENET BULGAN

ÖLGIY

ALTAI TAVAN BOGD NATIONAL PARK

HAR NUUR

STUPAS Buddhist religious structures

KHANGAI MOUNTAINS

ERDENE ZUU Buddhist monastery

ALTAI SNOWCOCK

HOVD

HAR US NUUR

ULIASTAY

KARAKORUM

BAATAR HAIRKHAN MOUNTAINS

YAK

ORKHON

BEECH MARTEN

ALTAI MOUNTAINS

ALTAY

STONE WALL surrounding the monastery

HORSE BREEDING

CATTLE

GOATS

HIKING

DEMOISELLE CRANE

LESSER SAND PLOVER

SIBERIAN CHIPMUNK

SIBERIAN IBEX

ALTAI MOUNTAINS

NARANBAATAR

BOLORMAA

GOLDEN EAGLE

OVOO a stone cairn dedicated to the divinities

SAXAUL

KHATA a traditional scarf given as a present or offered to the divinities

SPEAR GRASS

0 50 100 150 200 kilometers
0   50   100 miles

famous THROAT SINGING

BUNCHUK a symbol of power → moon → sun → horse-tail hair

HORSEBACK RIDING

Mongolia

♔ CAPITAL: ULAN BATOR

🍄 LANGUAGE: MONGOLIAN

👥 POPULATION: 3 MILLION

AREA: 1,564,116 KM² / 603,908 SQ. MI.

Монгол улс the country's name in Mongolian, written in traditional Mongolian script and in Cyrillic

GHENGIS KHAN ruler and founder of the Mongol empire in the 13th century

BUILDING A YURT: ①

FISHING

FEMALE ARCHER

MONGOLIAN WRESTLING

SHAGAI
the anklebones
of a sheep or goat
used as DICE

KHUUSHUUR
meat mixed
with onion or garlic,
fried in dough

BUUZ
a kind of meat
dumpling

TAIMEN

WRESTLER

HORSE RACES

ROAST MUTTON
is a staple
of the Mongolian diet.

AIRAG
fermented
horse
milk

BOORCOG
fried pastry served
as a dessert
with sugar,
butter, or honey

During NAADAM,
a traditional sports festival,
competitions are held
in three disciplines:
wrestling, horse racing,
and archery.

AMARBAYASGALANT
BUDDHIST
MONASTERY

ENGA

TURTLE-SHAPED
ROCK

WILD BOAR

GURILTAI SOUP
with meat
and handmade noodles

SUUTEI TSAI
salty tea
with milk

PARLIAMENT
BUILDING

GANDAN
Buddhist
monastery

CHOYBALSAN

STEPPE ①

SHEEP

ULAN BATOR

GORKHI-TERELJ
NATIONAL PARK

MONGOLIAN
GAZELLE

TUUL

POTATOES

BARLEY

WHEAT

STEPPE
AGAMA

STEPPE
MARMOT

tourists

40-METER/130-FOOT-HIGH
STATUE OF GHENGIS KHAN

KHAMAR
BUDDHIST
MONASTERY

MONGOLIAN
WILD ASS

GOITERED
GAZELLE

CAMEL
BREEDING

GREAT JERBOA

SAIGA
ANTELOPE

GOBI BEAR

Gobi Desert

BUDDHIST
WORLD ENERGY
CENTER

legendary monster
of the Gobi Desert,
the MONGOLIAN
DEATH
WORM

MONGOLIAN
HAT

DEEL

BAYANZAG
picturesque cliffs
and rocks

CORSAC FOX

PRZEWALSKI'S
HORSE

BACTRIAN
two-humped
camel

MONGOLIAN
BOOTS

DINOSAUR
FOSSILS
have been
found in
the Gobi Desert.

petrified
DINOSAUR EGGS
found in
the Gobi Desert

YURT
a traditional
Mongolian tent

ON A CAMEL

MONGOLS
IN TRADITIONAL
COSTUMES

WONTON
dumplings filled with
meat or shrimp

MAPO DOUFU
a dish of tofu with meat
in a spicy sauce

SICHUAN
PEPPER

WOK

SILKWORMS
feed on mulberry leaves.

MULBERRY LEAF

SILKWORM'S
COCOON

SILK

Then they wrap
themselves in a cocoon,
from which the fiber
to make silk
is acquired.

SILK MOTH

CENTURY EGG
eggs preserved
for several weeks
in a special mixture

DIM SUM

CHINESE
NOODLES

CONFUCIUS
great philosopher

MARBLED
POLECAT

CHINESE WOMAN
WEARING
A TRADITIONAL
CHEONGSAM

TEA

STINKY
TOFU

ACUPUNCTURE
a method of healing
that involves inserting
needles into the body

ALTAI

TIAN SHAN

TOFU
curd made with
soy milk

MEAT IN SWEET-
AND-SOUR SAUCE

tofu marinated
in a fermented sauce
made with meat,
milk, or vegetables

CHINESE MOUNTAIN CAT

CAVES OF
THE THOUSAND
BUDDHAS
temples carved
in the cliffs

TAI CHI

KUNG FU

Taklimakan
Desert

MASK
FROM THE
TIBETAN
OPERA

PING-
PONG

TIBETAN
WOLF

PAMIRS

KARAKORAM RANGE

KUNLUN RANGE

Tibet

KIANG

YAK
RACES

PRAYER
WHEELS

BUDDHIST
MONK
②

K2
8,611 meters /
28,250 ft.,
the second
highest peak
on earth

TSAMPA
roasted barley
flour

THUKPA
soup with vegetables
and noodles

TIBETAN
TEA
with yak butter
and salt

CHINESE
PADDLEFISH

LANTERN

HIMALAYAN
TAHR

TIBETAN
SAND FOX

MOMO
meat
dumplings

HIMALAYAS

POTALA
PALACE

•LHASA
②

CHINESE
DRAGON

TAIJITU
a symbol representing
the two primal forces,
yin and yang

CLIMBING
the highest peak
in the world.

the country's name
written in Chinese

CHO OYU /
8,153 meters /
26,750 ft.

CHOMOLUNGMA
or MOUNT EVEREST
8,848 meters / 29,028 ft.,
the highest peak on earth

LHOTSE
8,511 meters /
27,923 ft.

MAKALU
8,481 meters /
27,824 ft.

TIBETAN
ANTELOPE

PLANTING
RICE

GOLDEN
PHEASANT

CHINESE
PANGOLIN

GOLDEN
SNUB-NOSED
MONKEY

CHINA

中國

👑 CAPITAL: BEIJING

👅 LANGUAGES: MANDARIN,
as well as Cantonese, Shanghainese,
and many others

POPULATION: 1 BILLION
343 MILLION

AREA: 9,596,961 KM²/
3,705,407 SQ. MI.

GINKGO
LEAVES

MOON
BEAR

CHINESE
ALLIGATOR

PICKING
TEA

DAWN
REDWOOD

0   250   500 kilometers
0   250 miles

MONKS FROM SHAOLIN MONASTERY

RAT

SOME CHINESE INVENTIONS:

FIREWORKS

KITE

PORCELAIN

GUNPOWDER

MATCHES

PAPER

THE GAME OF GO

MANDARIN DUCK

CHINESE GOOSE

LI

WEI

GINSENG

ICE SCULPTURE FESTIVAL

JI LE BUDDHIST TEMPLE

ACTORS FROM THE CHINESE OPERA

① HANGING TEMPLE carved into the cliffs

HARBIN

SORGHUM

PEACHES

WATERMELONS

Manchuria

GREAT WALL OF CHINA

THE FORBIDDEN CITY former imperial palace

MUKDEN PALACE

SHENYANG

Gobi Desert

NATIONAL STADIUM

DATONG ①

BEIJING

TIANJIN

PEKINGESE

YUNGANG GROTTOES

TAI SHAN the sacred mountain of Taoism

YELLOW SEA

QINGHAI SALINE LAKE

YELLOW RIVER

POTATOES

TERRA-COTTA ARMY

WHEAT

SHANGHAI WORLD FINANCIAL CENTER

JIN MAO TOWER

ORIENTAL PEARL TOWER

JIUZHAIGOU VALLEY NATURE RESERVE

GIANT PANDA

YELLOW CRANE TOWER

PEANUTS

XI'AN

YUYUAN GARDEN

SHANGHAI

EAST CHINA SEA

TREPANGS, also known as SEA CUCUMBERS

YANGTZE

WUHAN

CHENGDU

LESHAN

CHONGQING

TEA

CANTON TOWER 600 meters / 1,968 ft. high

LESHAN GIANT BUDDHA the world's largest stone Buddha (71 meters / 233 ft. high)

LIMESTONE HILLS

TEMPLE OF THE SIX BANYAN TREES

CHINESE WHITE DOLPHIN

TERRACED FIELDS in which rice is grown

RICE

GUILIN

GUANGZHOU

HONG KONG

XI

BAMBOO

CATCHING FISH WITH A CORMORANT

SUNNY BEACHES

Hainan

SOUTH CHINA SEA

DRAGON BOAT RACE

DRAGON DANCE and LION DANCE — Chinese New Year traditions

49

YAK

CHOUGH

THE HIMALAYAS ARE THE WORLD'S HIGHEST MOUNTAINS.

THE EYES OF BUDDHA
a Buddhist religious symbol

NAMASTE!
the traditional words and gesture of greeting used in Nepal and India

Above a height of 4,800 meters / 15,700 feet in the Himalayas, the snow never melts

MAGNOLIA

MADAL drum

LAPSI FRUITS

SLOTH BEAR

BUDDHIST STUPA
a religious structure

ROYAL PALACE

LO MANTHANG

POTATOES

TSARANG

HIKING IN THE MOUNTAINS

KARNALI

CHITAL DEER

DHANGADHI

DHAULAGIRI,
or White Mountain,
8,172 meters / 26,810 ft.

ANNAPURNA
8,078 meters
26,504 ft.

MILLET

THE TERAI
lowland terrain at the foot of the Himalayas

SUGAR CANE

VILLAGE

POKHARA

DINGHY RIDES

PHEWA LAKE

A WOMAN CARRYING WOOD

TULSIPUR

GAUR

STREET SELLER

SANDALWOOD TREE

LUMBINI
Buddha's birthplace

selling colored dyes, used in Hindu religious ceremonies

SANDALWOOD FRUITS AND LEAVES

PEACOCK ORCHID

BARLEY

BANANA TREE

BAMBOO

CORCHORUS
(jute)

RHODODENDRON
the national flower of Nepal

HIMALAYAN MONAL
the national bird of Nepal

SUNDARI
is a Nepali name meaning "beautiful."

CORN

WATER BUFFALO

NEPAL

नेपाल

↑ the country's name in Nepali

Nepal is home to many species of BUTTERFLIES.

INDIAN ELEPHANT

👑 CAPITAL: KATHMANDU

👅 LANGUAGES: NEPALI
as well as Maithili, Bhojpuri, Tharu, Tamang, and many others

DAWA
is a Sherpa name meaning "moon"

BENGAL TIGER

👥👥👥 POPULATION: 30 MILLION

⤢ AREA: 147,181 KM² / 56,827 SQ. MI.

DAL BHAT TARKARI
soup made with lentils, rice, and curried vegetables

0   25   50 kilometers
0   25 miles

50

SNOW LEOPARD

ALTAI ARGALI

ICE AX

CLIMBING ROPE

THE SHERPAS are a people who live high up in the Himalayas. Since Himalayan mountaineering began, the Sherpas have helped climbers scale the highest peaks as guides and bearers.

PRAYER FLAGS

hung up by Tibetan Buddhists

YETI a legendary creature that lives in the Himalayas

HIMALAYAN GORAL

FOOTPRINTS OF THE YETI?

HIMALAYAN MOUNTAINEERS' CAMP

In 1950 the French climbers Maurice Herzog and Louis Lachenal became the first climbers to reach the summit of Annapurna, at 8,078 meters / 26,504 feet.

The first men to climb to the top of Mount Everest, which happened in 1953

Sherpa TENZING NORGAY

New Zealander EDMUND HILLARY

TENZING ON THE PEAK OF EVEREST

The Poles Krzysztof Wielicki and Leszek Cichy were the first men to climb Mount Everest in winter.

YAK CARAVAN with mountaineers' luggage

Above 8,000 meters / 26,000 feet, the air is very thin, so most mountaineers use OXYGEN CANISTERS.

CRAMPONS are special spikes fixed to boots for walking on ice and snow while mountaineering.

MANASLU 8,161 meters / 26,775 ft.

SWAYAMBHUNATH TEMPLE known as the Monkey Temple

PASHUPATINATH TEMPLE a sacred Hindu site

CHO OYU 8,153 meters / 26,750 ft.

CHOMOLUNGMA or MOUNT EVEREST 8,848 meters / 29,028 ft, the highest peak on earth

KANGCHENJUNGA 8,586 meters / 28,169 ft, the third highest peak on earth

BANDIPUR

TRISHULI

KATHMANDU

BHAKTAPUR

PATAN

DURBAR SQUARE

BOUDHANATH huge Buddhist stupa

NAMCHE BAZAAR

LHOTSE 8,511 meters / 27,923 ft, the fourth highest peak on earth

MAKALU 8,481 meters / 27,824 ft, the fifth highest peak on earth

LUKLA

CHITWAN NATIONAL PARK

RURAL COTTAGE

SUN KOSI

DHARAN

RHESUS MONKEY

SAL TREE

JANAKI MANDIR Hindu temple

KINGFISHER

TEA

CLOUDED LEOPARD

RICE

MUGGER CROCODILE

JANAKPUR

MOUNTAIN BIKING

WHEAT

NILGAI

BIRATNAGAR

INDIAN RHINOCEROS

RED PANDA

WOMEN AT WORK

India

भारत ← the country's name, written in Hindi

- **CAPITAL: NEW DELHI**
- **LANGUAGES: HINDI, ENGLISH,** and many others spoken regionally
- **POPULATION: 1 BILLION 210 MILLION**
- **AREA: 3,287,263 KM²/ 5,269,219 SQ. MI.**

kilometers
0 50 100 150 200 250
0   50   100 miles

INDIAN ELEPHANT

INDIAN WILD DOG

CAMELS are bred in India.

DECORATED ELEPHANT

HIMALAYAS

PATKAI RANGE

BRAHMAPUTRA

SOUTH ASIAN RIVER DOLPHIN

HINDU DANCERS

CRICKET

INDIAN STICK INSECT

INDIAN COBRA

URIAL

DOSA very thin pancakes

CHUTNEY a popular condiment, served with all sorts of dishes

TEA

WOMAN PICKING TEA

FIELD HOCKEY

ORANGES

RASAM a soup, made with juice from tamarind fruit

PEAS, BEANS, and LENTILS are popular. In India, peas, beans, and lentils are popular.

BANYAN TREE

NAAN bread

CHICKEN TIKKA pieces of chicken cooked in a tandoor, oven with sauce

CURRY vegetables or meat in a sauce made with a mixture of spices

KANGCHENJUNGA 8,586 meters / 28,169 ft, the highest peak in India.

GANGES

MAHABODHI BUDDHIST TEMPLE

INDIAN PEACOCK

GREEN MAGPIE

INDIAN RHINOCEROS

TANDOORI OVEN

MASALA CHAI tea with milk and spices

HIMALAYAS

THE TAJ MAHAL MAUSOLEUM

BATHING IN THE GANGES a river sacred to Hindus

KANPUR

YAMUNA

SARUS CRANE

INDUS

AGRA

SUGAR CANE

WHEAT

TIGER

In India, COWS are regarded as sacred animals.

THE INDIA GATE

LOTUS TEMPLE

NEW DELHI

MADHYA RANGE

CHICKPEA

CORN

LOTUS FLOWER

MANGO

leaves and fruits of the TAMARIND

GOLDEN TEMPLE

ASIATIC LION

Thar Desert

GREAT INDIAN BUSTARD

RAHUL

ADITI

KURTA

WOMAN IN A SARI

DHOTI

GHARIAL

YOGA

WATER BUFFALO

BRAHMINY KITE

BLACK-HEADED BULBUL

NICOBAR PIGEON

Nicobar Islands

Andaman Islands

CALCUTTA

RICKSHAW

BAY OF BENGAL

GIANT BARRACUDA

BONITO

BRYDE'S WHALE

VICTORIA MEMORIAL

MOON WRASSE

RICE

BLUE-THROATED BARBET

EASTERN GHATS

THE LION-TAILED MONKEY

CRIMSON SUNBIRD

BONNET MACAQUE

KAPALEESHWARAR TEMPLE

MADRAS

BRIHADEESWARAR TEMPLE AT THANJAVUR

SATPURA RANGE

COTTON

CHARMINAR mosque

HYDERABAD

FOXTAIL MILLET

SORGHUM

VIDHANA SOUDHA

BANGALORE

PURPLE FROG

INDIAN OCEAN

COCONUTS

TEMPLES AT ELLORA

AHMADABAD

SURAT

PUNE

WESTERN GHATS

LION-TAILED MACAQUE

PINK SKUNK CLOWNFISH

PEANUTS

THE GATEWAY OF INDIA

MUMBAI

SHANIWAR WADA FORT

BEACH

COCONUT PALM

Lakshadweep Islands

MAHATMA GANDHI was a famous Indian leader and wise man.

ARABIAN SEA

53

Thailand

CAPITAL: BANGKOK
LANGUAGE: THAI
POPULATION: 67 MILLION
AREA: 513,120 KM.²/ 198,117 SQ. MI.

ประเทศไทย
the country's name written in Thai

KASEM

PAVEENA

FLYING DRAGON

WORKING IN A RICE FIELD

RANAT EK

RIDING AN ELEPHANT

SIAMESE CAT

RETICULATED PYTHON

ELEPHANT SCHOOL

WOMAN FROM THE KAREN PEOPLE

BEAR CAT

SUN BEAR

CRAB-EATING MACAQUE

BANTENG

PURPLE MANGOSTEEN

MEKONG

GOLDEN SHOWER TREE BLOSSOM
Thailand's national flower

JASMINE RICE

MANIOC

RICE

UBON RATCHATHANI

UDON THANI

KHON KAEN

PHANOM RUNG TEMPLE

NAKHON RATCHASIMA

STATUE OF LADY MO

THE GRAND PALACE

KHAO YAI NATIONAL PARK

colorful insect LANTERN BUG

SNAKEHEAD MURREL

PHITSANULOK

TA SAK

WAT ARUN

WAT PHRA SRI SANPHET

BANGKOK ①

MENAM

BANGKOK ②

THA CHIN

WAT PHRA THAT DOI SUTHEP

VILLAGE

CHIANG RAI

CURVED SPINY SPIDER

NAN

YOM

PING

RUINS OF THE HISTORIC CITY OF SUKHOTHAI

AYUTTHAYA

NAKHON SAWAN

SUGAR CANE

NAKHON PATHOM

CHIANG MAI

DOI INTHANON
2,585 meters / 8,481 ft.
Thailand's highest peak

MAE KLONG

BRIDGE ON THE RIVER KWAI

CENTIPEDE

YOUNG TEAK TREE

RUBBER TREE

PINEAPPLE

CHILIS

TEAK TREE LEAF

SUNDA PANGOLIN

INDOCHINESE TIGER

TUK-TUK auto rickshaw
TAXI

THE EMERALD BUDDHA ①
a figure made of jadeite and gold
Thailand's national treasure

DANCERS

YOUNG BUDDHIST MONK

KAFFIR LIME FRUITS AND LEAVES

RAMBUTAN

CHILDREN IN SCHOOL UNIFORMS

SEPAK TAKRAW
a rattan ball for games

KRABI KRABONG
a traditional Thai martial art

TOM YUM
spicy soup with seafood or chicken

NAM PLA
fish sauce

BAMBOO SHOOTS

MUAY THAI
Thai boxing

PAD THAI
fried rice noodles with lots of spices and added extras

SNACKS MADE OF INSECTS

THAI EGGPLANTS

SUNDA FLYING LEMUR

LEMUR IN FLIGHT

SALTWATER CROCODILE

IRRAWADDY DOLPHIN

RED LIONFISH

SUNDA SLOW LORIS

DURIAN
a very stinky fruit

Ko Kut

Ko Chang

Ko Phangan

Ko Samui

FLOATING MARKET

GULF OF THAILAND

TUNA

FLASK-SHAPED PITCHER PLANTS
insect-eating plants

BEACH

SHRIMP

BOAT

HAT YAI

SONGKHLA

MOONRAT

PATTAYA

NAKHON SI THAMMARAT

FRUIT SELLER

Ko Tarutao

SURAT THANI

COCONUTS

TEMPLE

MALAYAN TAPIR

WHITE-HANDED GIBBON

WHITE-BELLIED SEA EAGLE

KHAO SOK NATIONAL PARK

Ko Phuket

RAI LEH PENINSULA

RAFFLESIA
an enormous flower

ANDAMAN SEA

RED-CROWNED CRANE

BROWN BEAR

RED FOX

DAISETSUZAN NATIONAL PARK

●SAPPORO

huge SNOW SCULPTURES at the festival in Sapporo

Rishiri

Rebun

Hokkaido

SAMURAI

NINJA Japanese warrior

GUNDAM giant robot from films and cartoons

KATANA traditional Japanese sword

MAPLES

RANCHU goldfish

KOI CARP

SAKURA blossoming cherry tree

TOKYO TOWER

MATSUMOTO CASTLE

Honshu

Sado

BASEBALL is very popular in Japan.

KENDO

TRADITIONAL THEATER MASK

MANGA famous Japanese comics

PERSIMMONS

STRAWBERRIES

TOFU is bean curd made with soy milk

KARAOKE comes from Japan.

HUGE JELLYFISH

SHRIMP

OYSTERS

SEA OF JAPAN

SUMO WRESTLERS

TEMPURA seafood and vegetables dipped in batter and deep-fried.

GREEN TEA

SOYBEANS

ORIGAMI

AIKIDO

WORKING IN A RICE FIELD

Pressed NORI SEAWEED is a basic ingredient of sushi.

DAIKON Japanese radish

IKEBANA the art of flower arranging

JUDO

RICE is a staple of the Japanese diet

SOY SAUCE

BONSAI TREE

KENJUTSU a martial art with swords

JAPANESE ZEN GARDEN

SUSHI is a dish made with rice, seaweed, seafood, and vegetables.

WASABI very hot Japanese plant, also known as horseradish

RAMEN is Japanese chicken soup with noodles.

SAKE alcohol distilled from rice

MISO SOUP

TEA CEREMONY

MATCHA powdered green tea

BAMBOO TREE

Japan

CAPITAL: TOKYO

LANGUAGE: JAPANESE

POPULATION: 128 MILLION

AREA: 377,915 KM² / 145,913 SQ. MI.

日本 ← the country's name in Japanese

MISAKI   AKIRA

CALLIGRAPHY
the art of beautiful handwriting

GODZILLA
a monster from films

JAPANESE WOMEN IN KIMONOS

KIMONO
traditional Japanese robe

ZŌRI
sandals

SCHOOLGIRL IN UNIFORM

GETA
wooden sandals

CHERRY BLOSSOM

FANS

CHRYSANTHEMUMS

STATUE OF BUDDHA
in the town of Kamakura

SHINJUKU DISTRICT

The Japanese produce world-famous CARS AND MOTORBIKES.

The Japanese produce world-famous of ELECTRONICS.

A GEISHA entertains guests at parties with singing, dancing, playing traditional Japanese instruments, and calligraphy, among other Japanese arts.

SAMISEN
a three-stringed instrument

JAPANESE SPIDER CRAB
Its leg span can reach four meters / 12 feet.

Japan is one of the world's major producers

TAKIFUGU
puffs itself up in case of danger

TŌ-JI
Buddhist pagoda

MOUNT FUJI
an active volcano

MOUNT FUJI 3,776 meters / 12,388 feet Japan's highest peak

TOKYO
KAWASAKI
YOKOHAMA

NAGOYA

KYOTO

OSAKA

KOBE

PAGODA KONPON-DAITŌ

KAMO SHRINE
Shinto temple

HIMEJI CASTLE

KOTOHIRA-GU TEMPLE

PACIFIC OCEAN

TUNA

PACIFIC COD

MACKEREL

KARATE
Karate originated on Okinawa.

Okinawa

RYUKYU ISLANDS

CORAL REEFS

Miyako

Ishigaki

Iriomote

MANEKI-NEKO
a figurine that brings good luck

JAPANESE CEDAR

SHINKANSEN
high-speed Japanese train that travels at up to 300 km/h / 186 mph

HIROSHIMA

TORII

120-meter / 390-foot-high FERRIS WHEEL

FUKUOKA

Shikoku

Kyushu

ASO VOLCANO

SENGAN-EN GARDEN

NAGASAKI

ONE-LEGGED TORII GATE

JAPANESE GIANT SALAMANDER

JAPANESE MACAQUE

Tsushima

Shimoshima

Tanegashima

Yakushima

Kuchinoerabu

Satsunan Islands

Takeshima

Ryukyu Islands
(In the box you can see the rest of the archipelago, which continues to the southwest.)

Kikai
Amami Ōshima
Tokunoshima

AMAMI RABBIT

kilometers   100
miles   50

57

Jordan is a desert country, and only some areas are suitable for CULTIVATION. The best arable land lies along the river Jordan.

BARLEY
WHEAT
LENTILS
OLIVE TREE
CHICKPEAS
MARKET
OUD
REBAB

EGGPLANT
CUCUMBERS
OLIVES
BANANAS
TOMATOES
PISTACHIO NUTS
PISTACHIO SPRIG

MELONS
SHEEP
GOATS

KING ABDULLAH I MOSQUE
IRBID
HADRIAN'S ARCH
JERASH

JORDAN

ROMAN THEATER

There is so much salt in the Dead Sea that a person's body floats on the water without sinking.

AZ-ZARQA
AR-RUSAYFAH
AMMAN
① MA'DABA
RUINS OF THE TEMPLE OF HERCULES

QASR' AMRA desert castle

Syria

The Dead Sea lies at the lowest point on earth, 418 meters / 1,302 feet below sea level

The water in the sea is so salty that no plants or animals live in it.

DEAD SEA

QASR AL-KHARANAH

MUD FROM THE DEAD SEA has medicinal properties.

SALT
FIGS
FIG LEAVES

AL-KARAK
KERAK Crusader castle

SHEPHERD

SCORPION

ROYAL POINCIANA

AT-TAFILA

AL KHAZNEH a building carved out of rock

DANA BIOSPHERE RESERVE

DATES

DATE PALM

Petra
site of the ruins of an ancient city

● MA'AN

BALLOON FLIGHT over Wadi Rum

WADI RUM a valley among picturesque rocks ②

AQABA
BEACH

JABAL UMM AD DAMI (MOUNT RAMM)
1,754 meters
Jordan's highest peak
1,754 m / 5,755 ft.

②

CLIMBING in Wadi Rum

BEDOUINS BREWING TEA

CORAL REEF

GULF OF AQABA

DIVER

CLIFF PAINTINGS in Wadi Rum

ONE-HUMPED CAMEL or DROMEDARY

BEETLE

ARABIAN HORSE

SOCCER is a popular sport in Jordan.

OLIVE OIL

KHUBZ BREAD

MANSAF
lamb cooked in yogurt, served with rice and almonds

KIBBEH
croquettes made with grain or rice and meat

HIJAB
a scarf covering the hair, ears, and neck of Muslim women

SPICE SELLER

TEA MADE WITH MINT OR SAGE

HUMMUS
a dish made with chickpeas, sesame paste, garlic, olive oil, and lemon juice

AGAL
secures the keffiyeh

KEFFIYEH
Arab headdress known in Jordan as a HATTAH

esert

venomous PALESTINE VIPER

DISHDASHA
traditional robe worn by Arab men

CITIZENS OF JORDAN

STRIPED HYENA

LESSER KESTREL

BLACK IRIS

MOSAIC MAP IN MADABA ①

ARABIAN WOLF

TOURING THE DESERT

HIKING

SINAI ROSEFINCH

GOLDEN JACKAL

HORSEBACK RIDING

SAND RAT

CAMEL RIDING

SHRAK
Bedouin bread

SAND CAT

SANDGROUSE

ROCK HYRAX

AHMAD

HALA

SINAI AGAMA

DESERT COBRA

ARABIAN ORYX

Bedouins cook meat and vegetables in an OVEN buried in the ground.

JORDAN

CARACAL

♔ CAPITAL: AMMAN

الأردن
the country's name written in Arabic

🗣 LANGUAGE: ARABIC

👤👤👤 POPULATION: 6.5 MILLION

AREA: 89,342 KM²/ 34,495 SQ. MI.

BEDOUIN TENT

NUBIAN IBEX

0   25   50 kilometers
0   25 miles

59

ATLANTIC
SPOTTED
DOLPHIN

Madeira
(Portugal)

Canary Islands
(Spain)

RABAT

ALGIERS

TUNISIA

TUNIS

TRIPOLI

MOROCCO

ALGERIA

MEDITERRANEAN
FLYING FISH

EL AAIÚN

WESTERN
SAHARA

MAURITANIA

MALI

NIGER

CAPE
VERDE

NOUAKCHOTT

PRAIA

DAKAR
BANJUL

SENEGAL
GAMBIA

BAMAKO

BURKINA
FASO

NIAMEY

N'DJAMENA

OUAGADOUGOU

GUINEA-BISSAU
BISSAU

GUINEA

BENIN

NIGERIA

ABUJA

ATLANTIC SAILFISH

CONAKRY
FREETOWN

SIERRA LEONE

MONROVIA
LIBERIA

GHANA
TOGO
LOMÉ

PORTO
NOVO

YAMOUSSOUKRO

ACCRA

CAMEROON

YAOUNDÉ

IVORY
COAST

EQUATORIAL
GUINEA
SÃO TOMÉ

MALABO

LIBREVILLE
GABON

LEATHERBACK
SEA TURTLE

SÃO TOMÉ
AND PRÍNCIPE

Pagalu
(Equatorial
Guinea)

REPUBLIC
BRAZZAVILLE
KINSH

Ascension Island
(United Kingdom)

LUANDA

PORTUGUESE
MAN O'WAR

St. Helena
(United Kingdom)

NAMIBIA

A T L A N T I C   O C E A N

WINDHOE

MANTA

60

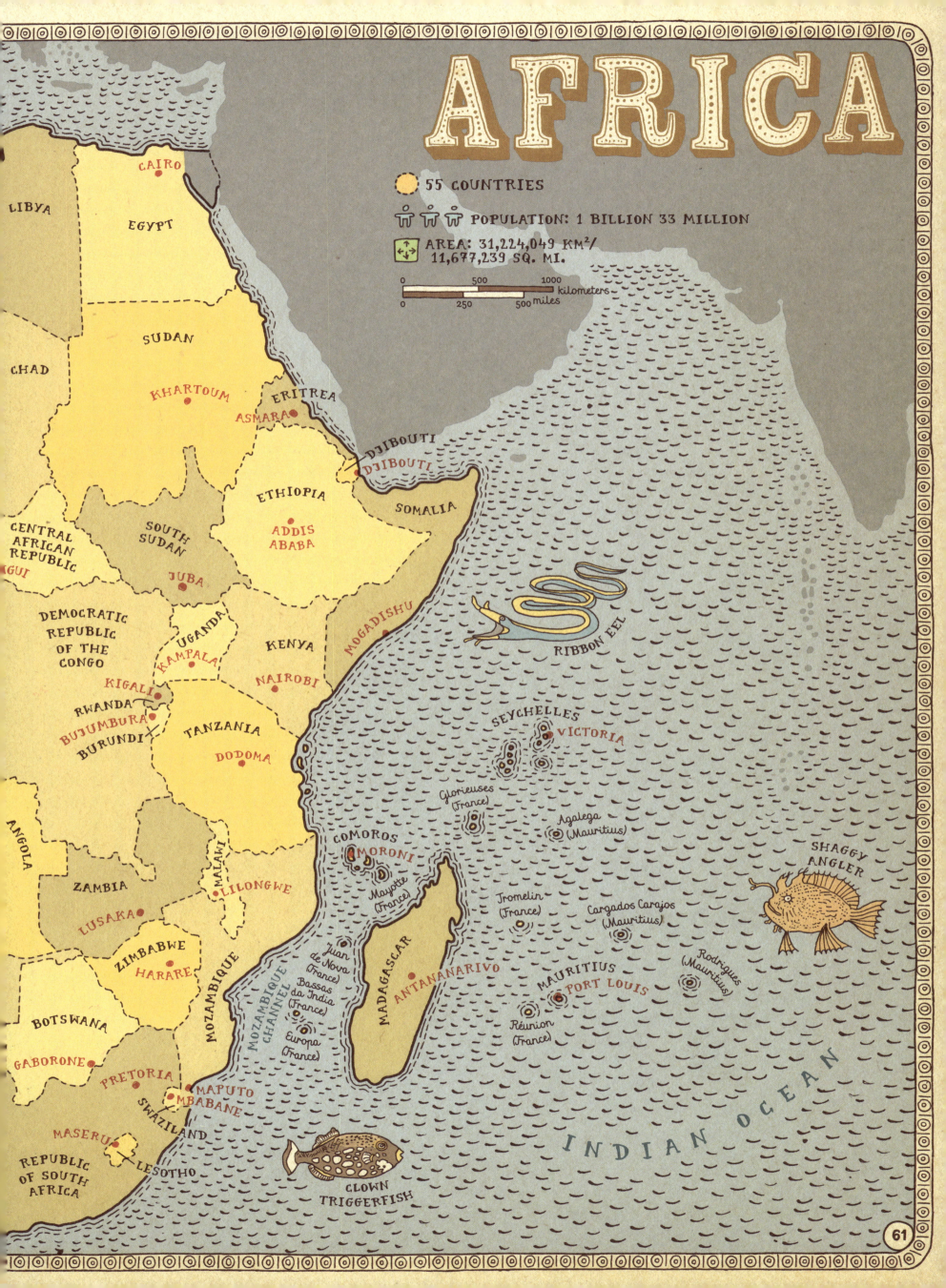

AFRICA

● 55 COUNTRIES

POPULATION: 1 BILLION 33 MILLION

AREA: 31,224,049 KM²/
11,677,239 SQ. MI.

500   1000
0   kilometers
0   250   miles
            500

LIBYA

EGYPT

CAIRO

CHAD

SUDAN

KHARTOUM

ERITREA

ASMARA

DJIBOUTI
DJIBOUTI

CENTRAL
AFRICAN
REPUBLIC

GUI

SOUTH
SUDAN

ETHIOPIA

ADDIS
ABABA

SOMALIA

JUBA

DEMOCRATIC
REPUBLIC
OF THE
CONGO

UGANDA

KAMPALA

KENYA

MOGADISHU

NAIROBI

KIGALI

RWANDA

BUJUMBURA

BURUNDI

TANZANIA

DODOMA

RIBBON EEL

SEYCHELLES

VICTORIA

Glorieuses
(France)

Agalega
(Mauritius)

ANGOLA

ZAMBIA

LUSAKA

MALAWI

LILONGWE

COMOROS

MORONI

Mayotte
(France)

Tromelin
(France)

Cargados Carajos
(Mauritius)

SHAGGY
ANGLER

ZIMBABWE

HARARE

MOZAMBIQUE

MOZAMBIQUE CHANNEL

Juan
de Nova
(France)

Bassas
da India
(France)

MADAGASCAR

ANTANANARIVO

MAURITIUS

PORT LOUIS

Rodrigues
(Mauritius)

BOTSWANA

Europa
(France)

Réunion
(France)

GABORONE

PRETORIA

MAPUTO

MBABANE

SWAZILAND

MASERU

LESOTHO

REPUBLIC
OF SOUTH
AFRICA

CLOWN
TRIGGERFISH

INDIAN OCEAN

MOROCCO

المغرب
↳ the country's name written in Arabic

👑 CAPITAL: RABAT

0 25 50 75 100 kilometers
25 50 miles

LANGUAGES: ARABIC, TAMAZIGHT (BERBER), and French

POPULATION: 32 MILLION

AREA: 446,550 KM² / 172,414 SQ. MI.

SAIDA MOHAMED

HARBOR PORPOISE

SARDINES

DATE PALM

GRAPEVINES

DATES

OLIVES

HAWKSBILL SEA TURTLE

FISHING BOAT

JEMAA EL-FNAA SQUARE

SHORT-FINNED PILOT WHALE

SKALA DU PORT BASTION

BEACH

TENSIFT

ATLANTIC OCEAN

BOATS IN THE PORT

ESSAOUIRA

MARRAKECH

ARGAN ②

ARGAN FRUITS

TOUBKAL
4,165 meters
13,665 ft.,
Morocco's
highest peak

TUNA

AGADIR TAROUDANT

SWORDFISH

RELAXING ON THE BEACH

FORTIFICATIONS

SAFFRON

BONITO

BARBARY FALCON

ANTI-ATLAS

GATEWAY TO THE CITY OF TAN-TAN

DESERT MONITOR

ZELLIGE
mosaics decorating
Moroccan buildings

FORTRESS IN THE OCEAN

DRAA

STRIPED HYENA

TARFAYA

NORTHERN BALD IBIS

AFRICAN WILDCAT

62

MEDITERRANEAN SEA

CEUTA (Spain)

TANGIER

TÉTOUAN

MELILLA (Spain)

ORANGES

HOUSES IN CHEFCHAOUEN

RIF MOUNTAINS

MANDRAGORA OFFICINARUM

ROYAL PALACE GATE

HASSAN TOWER

BARLEY

WHEAT

GATEWAY

OUJDA

SÉBOU

BAB BOU JELOUD, The Blue Gate

BAB AL-MANSUR GATE

AL-QARAWIYYIN MOSQUE

COMMON GENET

KENITRA

SALÉ

RABAT

CHELLAH

FEZ ①

SHEEP

CASABLANCA

MEKNÈS

BAHT

BOU REGREG

CATTLE

MIDDLE ATLAS

RED-BILLED CHOUGH

GOLDEN JACKAL

HASSAN II MOSQUE

OUM ER-RBIA

MOULOUYA

SCORPION

TOMATOES

OUZOUD WATERFALLS

TODGHA GORGE

BARBARY MACAQUE

DESERT HEDGEHOG

SNAKE CHARMER

ATLAS

TINGHIR

AIT BENHADDOU fortified village

ERG CHEBBI a desert with huge dunes

DESERT CAMP

LEATHER TANNING ①

OUARZAZAT

KASBAH TAOURIRT fortress

WHITE STORK

RIDING A CAMEL

ELEPHANT SHREW

DRAA

GARAGAB metal instrument

BALGHA leather footwear

BARBARY SHEEP

DJELLABA

DJELLABA a robe worn by men and women

MINT

②

MAKING ARGAN OIL

ALMONDS

GREEN TEA WITH MINT

KAFTAN

DAMA GAZELLE

COUSCOUS

SOUK an Arab market

TAGINE meat and vegetables cooked in a special pot of the same name

PASTILLA

COUSCOUS WITH VEGETABLES

KHUBZ

TAGINE

SERVING TEA

meat pie

bread

63

Egypt

مصر
the country's name written in Arabic

Gold mask from the tomb of **TUTANKHAMEN**

CAPITAL: CAIRO

LANGUAGE: ARABIC

0 — 50 — 100 kilometers
0 — 25 — 50 miles

POPULATION: 84 MILLION

AREA: 1,001,450 KM²/ 386,662 SQ. MI.

MEDITERRANEAN SE

FIGS

SCORPION

EL ALAMEIN

SCARAB BEETLE
Scarabs roll manure into balls.
In ancient Egypt it was regarded as a sacred insect.

DATE PALM

MOUNTAIN OF THE DEAD
a hill covered in tombs
SIWA OASIS

OLIVE TREE

BAHARIYA OASIS

DECORATED SARCOPHAGUS OF A PHARAOH

MUMMY
in an open sarcophagus

PHARAOH
a ruler of ancient Egypt

DATES

CLEOPATRA
the last queen of ancient Egypt

ANTLION

WHITE DESERT

QASR AL-FARAFRA

PAPYRUS SEDGE
Its fibers were used to make **PAPYRUS**, material on which people wrote in ancient times.

EGYPTIAN MONGOOSE

PERFUMES and scented oils have been an Egyptian specialty for centuries.

TAMARISK

W e s t e

In ancient Egypt **CATS** were worshipped.

PEREGRINE FALCON

DROMEDARY - ONE-HUMPED CAMEL

The greater part of the country is covered with **DESERTS**; they are part of the **SAHARA**, the world's biggest desert.

DAKHLA OASIS

NUBIAN IBEX

EGYPTIAN JERBOA

EGYPTIAN COBRA

HORNED VIPER

FENNEC

SAND CAT

LONG-EARED HEDGEHOG

D e s e

CARAVAN

ANCIENT EGYPTIAN GODS

RA
god of the sun and creator of the world

THOTH
god of the moon and wisdom

OSIRIS
god of death and the afterlife

ISIS
goddess of fertility and magic

HORUS
god of heaven and guardian of the pharaohs

SET
god of storms, darkness, and chaos

GILF KEBIR PLATEAU

PREHISTORIC PETROGLYPHS

BIBLIOTHECA ALEXANDRINA library and cultural center

NILE DELTA

RICE

PORT SAID

ALEXANDRIA

PYRAMID OF CHEOPS
PYRAMID OF KHAFRE
PYRAMID OF KAURE

CAIRO TOWER

MOHAMMED ALI BASHA MOSQUE

GIZA

CAIRO

SAQQARA

SPHINX

SUEZ

THE SUEZ CANAL links the Red Sea and the Mediterranean Sea. It was built to save ships sailing between Europe and Asia from having to go around Africa.

EL FAIYUM

STEP PYRAMID OF DJOSER

Sinai Peninsula

BEDOUINS

KARKADE hibiscus tea

MUHAMMED

ASMAA

sweet TEA made with mint leaves

JUNGLE CAT

KUSHARI a dish made with rice, lentils, chickpeas, noodles, garlic, and tomato juice

FALAFEL fried croquettes made with chickpeas or beans

EGYPTIAN BREAD

BABA GANOUSH a dip made with eggplant and sesame

FUL MEDAMES a dish made with beans, olive oil, onion, garlic, and lemon juice

GEBEL KATHERINA 2,629 meters / 8,652 ft., Egypt's highest peak

ST. CATHERINE'S MONASTERY

MOUNT SINAI

ORANGES

EGYPTIAN MEN AND WOMEN

BEANS

COTTON

SUGAR BEETS

ONIONS

CORN

Crops are grown on irrigated land along the Nile.

CRUDE OIL EXTRACTION

WHEAT

SUGAR CANE

n

ASYUT

NILE one of the two longest rivers in the world (the other is the Amazon.)

SHARM AL-SHEIKH

STRAWBERRIES

SCUBA DIVER

CORAL REEF

SUNNY BEACHES

HURGHADA

ancient city

PRECINCT OF AMUN-RE

Eastern Desert

TITAN TRIGGERFISH

SEA GRASS

Thebes

KARNAK

LUXOR

VALLEY OF THE KINGS

EL-KHARGA

TEMPLE OF HIBIS

VALLEY OF THE QUEENS

THE COLOSSI OF MEMNON

HATSHEPSUT'S TEMPLE

IDFU

TEMPLE OF HORUS

HUMPHEAD WRASSE

EGYPTIAN LOTUS

ASWAN

HIGH DAM

ELECTRIC CATFISH

NUBIANS a people who live in southern Egypt

RED SEA

t

WILD BOAR

TEMPLE OF RAMESES II

LAKE NASSER

ABU SIMBEL

NILE CROCODILE

STEPPE EAGLE

DORCAS GAZELLE

HIEROGLYPHS – ancient Egyptian script

65

GHANA

CAPITAL: ACCRA

LANGUAGES: ENGLISH as well as Asantee, Ewe, and many others spoken regionally.

POPULATION: 25 MILLION

AREA: 238,533 KM² / 92,098 SQ. MI.

kilometers
0 25 50
0 25 miles

KWEBEN

AFI

PREPARING FUFU

THE AKAN PEOPLE make patterned fabric called KENTE.

GHANAIANS IN TRADITIONAL COSTUMES

AFRICAN PIED HORNBILL

OTI

ORANGE-CHEEKED WAXBILL

AARDVARK

PUFF ADDER

DAKA

SHEA FRUIT

TILAPIA

CROCODILE FROM THE TOWN OF PAGA

RED VOLTA

BOLGATANGA

SAVANNA an area of grassland with scattered trees

found in countries with a hot climate

SORGHUM

SHEA TREE

TAMALE

VILLAGE

SISSILI

GOLIATH HERON

WHITE VOLTA

KNOB-BILLED DUCK

KOB

BEAUTIFUL SUNBIRD

EDIBLE MANIOC

CRESTED PORCUPINE

MOLE NATIONAL PARK

LARABANGA MOSQUE

BOABENG-FIEMA MONKEY SANCTUARY

WA-NA CHIEF'S PALACE

WA

BAOBAB

COMMON DUIKER

BLACK VOLTA

ORIBI

HIPPOPOTAMUS

RED RIVER HOG

HONEY BADGER

AFRICAN ELEPHANT

PATAS MONKEY

① MARKET AT KUMASI

66

SOCCER is a popular sport in Ghana.

WLI FALLS

KPANLOGO DRUM

TOGO MOUNTAINS

MOUNT AFADJATO 885 metres, Ghana's highest mountain

• HO

NILE PERCH

FRUIT OF THE OIL PALM

VOLTA

PORT

INDEPENDENCE ARCH

KOFORIDUA

NATIONAL THEATER

ACCRA

TEMA

GULF OF GUINEA

HUMPBACK DOLPHIN

ATLANTIC BLUE MARLIN

FISHING BOATS

LAKE VOLTA

AFRICAN CLAWLESS OTTER

AFRICAN MANATEE

the world's biggest man-made lake

UMBRELLA ROCK

TERMITE MOUND termite colony

TSETSE FLY

DIAMONDS

HANGING BRIDGE AT KAKUM NATIONAL PARK

CASTLE

CAPE COAST

CANNONS AT THE CASTLE

CORN

TERMITES

PALACE

KUMASI ①

GOLD MINES

• OBUASI

ELMINA CASTLE

ELMINA

COTTON

TARO TUBERS

• SUNYANI

YAMS

COCOA PODS

COCOA BEANS

OIL PALM

SEKONDI-TAKORADI

TARO

SUGAR CANE

TROPICAL RAINFOREST

COCONUT PALMS

BEACH

TUNA

BANKU (corn dough) with RED RED (bean stew), fried plantains, and fish

FUFU a mash made with manioc and plantains or yams

KOLA NUTS

SOUP MADE WITH PALM NUTS

PALM OIL

CHIMPANZEE

NZULEZO VILLAGE ON THE WATER

67

CHEETAH

TSESSEBE

STRIPED HYENA

TEA

LAKE VICTORIA

NILE PERCH

MWANZA

Africa's biggest lake

SERENGETI NATIONAL PARK

AFRICAN ELEPHANT

SAFARI *tourists watching wild animals*

NILE CROCODILE

RICE

DIAMONDS

SAPPHIRES

RUBIES

NGORONGORO CRATER

LAKE EYASI *a salt lake*

BLACK MAMBA

OSTRICH

BABOON

CHIMPANZEE

BAOBAB FRUIT

BAOBAB

TERMITE

MILLET

ELAND

WHITE-BACKED VULTURE

GOMBE STREAM NATIONAL PARK

TERMITE MOUND *termite colony*

BLUE WILDEBEEST

GREATER FLAMINGO

SAVANNA

SORGHUM

GRANT'S GAZELLE

PLAINS ZEBRA

LEOPARD

LAKE TANGANYIKA

CORN

ACACIA

LAKE RUKWA *a salt lake*

RUAHA NATIONAL PARK

LIONESS WITH CUBS

WARTHOG

GIRAFFE

GREAT WHITE PELICAN

TSETSE FLY

ABASI

NEEMA

AFRICAN BUFFALO

SIDE-STRIPED JACKAL

MARABOU STORK

MBOZI METEORITE *one of the largest meteorites found on earth*

TOBACCO

LION

SPOTTED HYENA

LAKE NYASA

0   50   100 kilometers
  25   50 miles

TANZANIA

Tanzania ← *The country's name is spelled the same in Swahili and in English.*

CAPITAL: DODOMA

LANGUAGES: ENGLISH, SWAHILI, *and numerous local languages*

POPULATION: 44 MILLION

AREA: 947,300 KM²/ 365,755 SQ. MI

BLACK RHINOCEROS

HIPPOPOTAMUS

TAMARIND FRUIT

MAASAI VILLAGE

GIANT GROUNDSEL

MAASAI PEOPLE

PANDANUS

BANANAS

UGALI
corn-flour porridge, served with meat and vegetables

CHAI MAZIWA
tea with milk and spices

OL DOINYO LENGAI VOLCANO
MERU VOLCANO
ARUSHA

KILIMANJARO
5,895 meters | 19,341 ft., the highest peak in Tanzania and all Africa

GIRL CARRYING FIREWOOD

FISHERMEN

WOMEN AT WORK

LOGGERHEAD SEA TURTLE

CLOVES

INDIAN OCEAN

ROCK PAINTINGS AT KONDOA

WHEAT

COFFEE

TANGA

Pemba

SCUBA DIVING

DOLPHIN

PARLIAMENT BUILDING

FORMER SULTAN'S PALACE

BOATS

DODOMA

SIMBA HILL

MARKET AT KARIAKOO

Zanzibar

ZANZIBAR

SNORKELING

COTTON

DAR ES SALAAM

SISAL
This plant is the source of SISAL, strong fiber used to make ropes.

WHALE SHARK

ISIMILA
Stone Age tools and prehistoric animal bones were found here.

Mafia

TRUMPETFISH

WHITEMARGIN UNICORNFISH

RUFIJI

RUINS AT KILWA KISIWANI

SELOUS game reserve

STARFISH

CATTLE

CASHEWS

COCONUT PALMS

OCEAN SUNFISH

AFRICAN BLACKWOOD
Wood from this tree is used to make musical instruments.

COCONUT

TAMARIND

MANIOC

MASK OF THE MAKONDE PEOPLE
famous for their wood carving

KUNENE

EPUPA FALLS

WELWITSCHIA
This plant is capable of living for several hundred years.

SORGHUM

SHIPWRECKS on the Skeleton Coast

ADENIA PECHUELII
a plant known as elephant's foot

OSHAKATI

LAKE ETOSHA
a salt lake

ETOSHA NATIONAL PARK

TSUMEB

MOPANE

GROOTFONTEIN

HOBA METEORITE
the biggest meteorite found on earth

MOPANE LEAVES

Skeleton Coast

BROWN FUR SEAL

BRANDBERG
2,606 meters / 8,443 ft.
Namibia's highest peak

OTJIWARONGO

WATERBERG NATIONAL PARK

②

PYGMY SPERM WHALE

①

the peaks of SPITZKOPPE

PARLIAMENT BUILDING

GERMAN COLONIAL ARCHITECTURE

URANIUM ORE MINING

WINDHOEK

ORCA

SWAKOPMUND

WALVIS BAY

REHOBOTH

GREATER FLAMINGO

PERINGUEY'S DESERT ADDER

QUIVER TREE

ATLANTIC OCEAN

SARDINES

The world's highest sand dunes are found in Namibia. Some of them are as much as 300 meters / 984 ft. high.

ANCHOVIES

GECKO

SHEEP

AINA   ZEKA

PILOT FISH

ABANDONED TOWN
In the past, diamonds were mined here.

HAKE

COLONIAL ARCHITECTURE

LÜDERITZ

KEETMANSHOOP

50   100
kilometers
0
25   50
miles

KOLMANSKOP

Namibia

👑 CAPITAL: WINDHOEK

🗣 LANGUAGES: ENGLISH
also Afrikaans, German, and many Namibian indigenous people's languages

👥👥👥 POPULATION: 2 MILLION

Namibia
the country's name is spelled the same in German and English

Namibië
the country's name in Afrikaans

⬌⬍ AREA: 824,292 KM²/
318,261 SQ. MI.

AFRICAN PENGUIN

FISH RIVER CANYON one of the world's biggest

DIAMONDS

ORANGE

70

GONIMBRASIA BELINA MOTH and its edible caterpillars

VILLAGE HUTS

PEARL MILLET

ZAMBEZI

KATIMA MULILO

LECHWE

AFRICAN ELEPHANTS

RUNDU

CORN

MUDUMU NATIONAL PARK

GIRAFFE

ZEBRA

WOMEN OF THE HERERO PEOPLE

CATTLE

GREATER KUDU

HIPPOPOTAMUS

CARACAL

WOMAN FROM THE OVAMBO PEOPLE

LION

MOZAMBIQUE SPITTING COBRA

WOMEN AND CHILDREN OF THE HIMBA PEOPLE

SAVANNA

STORKS spend the winter in Namibia.

CHEETAH

GROUND PANGOLIN

AFRICAN WILD DOG

BROWN HYENA

LEOPARD TORTOISE

SAN ROCK PAINTINGS

① ②

DINOSAUR FOOTPRINTS preserved in rock

HAMERKOP

PYGMY FALCON

GEMSBOK

MEMBERS OF THE SAN PEOPLE

NARA FRUIT

KALAHARI DESERT

Namibia is home to many species of SCORPIONS.

BEETLES that live in the desert

SECRETARY BIRD

DASSIE RAT

BAT-EARED FOX

CHACMA BABOON

YELLOW MONGOOSE

AFRICAN FISH EAGLE

OSHIFIMA porridge made from pearl millet

PAP corn-flour porridge

QUAD BIKING OVER SAND DUNES

FLOWERS AND LEAVES OF THE QUIVER TREE

TOURING NAMIBIA

SANDBOARDING riding a board down sand dunes

MEAT WITH OSHIFIMA AND MUTETE LEAVES

SOUTHERN GROUND HORNBILL

COMMON GENET

GRAPEVINES

MEERKATS

SOUTHERN OSTRICH

BLACK MAMBA venomous snake

BLACK RHINOCEROS

71

REPUBLIC OF SOUTH AFRICA

Republiek van Suid-Afrika
→ the country's name in Afrikaans

iRiphabliki yaseNingizimu Afrika
→ the country's name in Zulu

〰 **CAPITAL: PRETORIA**

LANGUAGES: AFRIKAANS, ENGLISH, NDEBELE, PEDI, SOTO, SWATI, TSONGA, TSWANA, VENDA, XHOSA, ZULU

POPULATION: 49 MILLION

AREA: 1,219,090 KM² / 470,693 SQ. MI.

0   50   100   150   200   kilometers
0   50   100   miles

NELSON MANDELA — leader of the movement against apartheid

KING PROTEA

ACACIA KARROO

DESMOND TUTU — human-rights activist

① ANIMAL WATCHING FROM THE BACK OF AN ELEPHANT

SAN PEOPLE

LERATO   TEBOGO   JOHAN

RUGBY

CRICKET

KALAHARI DESERT

BRAAI — an African grill

BOBOTIE — spiced minced meat baked in an egg-based sauce

POTJIEKOS — meaning "a small pot of food"

BUNNY CHOW — meat or vegetables with curry sauce in hollowed-out bread

PACHYPODIUM NAMAQUANUM a plant known as "halfmens"

RICHTERSVELD NATIONAL PARK

AUGRABIES FALLS

ORANGE

HARU OMS — hut made of reeds by the NAMA PEOPLE

GIANT QUIVER TREE

CAPE MARIGOLD

EUPHORBIA

ROOIBOS tea

ROOIBOS FLOWERS

AFRICAN PENGUIN

GRAPEVINES

Northern Cape Province

Western Cape Province

NORTH WEST Province

CAPE COBRA

PEANUTS

SPRINGBOK

THE BIG HOLE diamond mine

SHORT-EARED ELEPHANT SHREW

KIMBERLEY

DIAMONDS

ORANGE

PUFF ADDER

PHYMATEUS MORBILLOSUS grasshopper

RIVERINE RABBIT

CHACMA BABOON

KAROO BUSTARD

COMMON BABOON SPIDER — venomous

ATLANTIC OCEAN

DIVING IN A CAGE AMID SHARKS

GREAT WHITE SHARK

CASTLE OF GOOD HOPE

BO-KAAP DISTRICT

TOWN HALL

Robben Island →

CAPE TOWN

MITCHELL'S PLAIN

TABLE MOUNTAIN

Cape of Good Hope

CAPE FOLD BELT

SHELLS with holes in them, found in Blombos Cave, are the oldest known jewelry, dating back 75,000 years

LIGHTHOUSE

Cape Agulhas, the southernmost point in Africa

ACACIA FLOWERS

CAPE VULTURE

RED-TAILED WIDOWBIRD

LIMPOPO

NILE CROCODILE

SAVANNA

LIMPOPO

POLOKWANE

KRUGER NATIONAL PARK

BAOBAB

MALACHITE SUNBIRD

③ SAN ROCK PAINTINGS

WHITE RHINOCEROS

IMPALA

PILANESBERG GAME RESERVE

VOORTREKKER MONUMENT

BLYDE RIVER CANYON

MBOMBELA

Mpumalanga

SORGHUM

LEOPARD TORTOISE

ZULU DANCERS

①

MAFIKENG

PRETORIA

Gauteng

② JOHANNESBURG

SOWETO

SOCCER CITY STADIUM

GOLD MINES

VAAL

"MRS. PLES" the skull of a human ancestor from two million years ago ②

④ THE ZULU live mainly in the KWAZULU-NATAL region.

CORN

WHEAT

At 948 meters / 3,110 feet high, this is the world's second highest complex of waterfalls.

CATCHING FISH

FISH TRAPS IN KOSI BAY

BLUE CRANE

PARLIAMENT of Free State Province

TUGELA FALLS

BLOEMFONTEIN

Free State

LESOTHO

TUGELA

SUGAR CANE

KwaZulu-Natal

CATTLE

③ MAFADI 3,450 meters / 11,320 ft., South Africa's highest peak

④ DURBAN

UMLAZI

BEACH

LEATHERBACK TURTLE

RISSO'S DOLPHIN

DRAKENSBERG

KNYSNA TURACO

Eastern Cape Province

GRAPEFRUIT

XHOSA VILLAGE

SOUTH AFRICAN ABALONE

ELEPHANT at the Addo Elephant National Park

EAST LONDON

SOUTHERN RIGHT WHALE

PORT ELIZABETH

SURFING

INDIAN OCEAN

MADAGASCAR

BLUE COUA

Many plants and animals are unique to Madagascar.

VANILLA

PARSON'S CHAMELEON

RED RUFFED LEMUR

GIRAFFE WEEVIL

RED FODY

ANTSIRANANA

COCOA PODS

LEAF-TAILED GECKO

HAIRY-EARED DWARF LEMUR

CLOVES

Nosy Boraha

DYSCOPHUS known as the tomato frog.

TOAMASINA

MAROMOKOTRO at 9436 ft., Madagascar's highest peak

LOWLAND STREAKED TENREC

LAKE ALAOTRA

TRAVELER'S PALM

SUGAR CANE

Nosy Be

COMMON BROWN LEMUR

QUEEN'S PALACE

ANTANANARIVO

MADAGASCAN DWARF CHAMELEON the second-smallest known chameleon

NILE CROCODILE

RED-TAILED SILVERSIDE

BETSIBOKA

PANTHER CHAMELEON

MAHAVAVY

RICE

MORAINGY traditional martial art

MADAGASCAR FISH EAGLE

HOOPOE

CAPITAL: ANTANANARIVO

LANGUAGES: MALAGASY, FRENCH

POPULATION: 22 MILLION

AREA: 587,041 KM²/ 226,658 SQ. MI

MADAGASIKARA

the country's name in Malagasy

INHABITANTS OF MADAGASCAR, THE MALAGASY

100 kilometers
50 miles
50
25
0

ANGONOKA TORTOISE

GRAY MOUSE LEMUR

MALAGASY PARADISE FLYCATCHER

TSINGY DE BEMARAHA pointed mountains

MADAGASCAR IBIS

KING PRAWN

ROYAL POINCIANA known as the flame tree

FLAME-TREE FLOWER

LANTONIAINA LALAINA

ZEBU

COMET ORCHID

MOZAMBIQUE CHANNEL

RAFFIA PALM

SISAL

BOAT

ORANGES

RAFFIA-PALM FRUIT

BANANAS

MANGOES

AKOHO SY VOANIO
chicken cooked in coconut milk

LAOKA
rice seasoned with ingredients such as peanuts and meat

KOBAN-DRAVINA
a dessert made with nuts and sugar cooked for a very long time in banana leaves

RANONAPANGO
a popular drink made by pouring boiling water on leftover burned rice

VALIHA
stringed instrument

BLACK MARLIN

BAMBARA PEANUTS

POTATOES

INDIAN OCEAN

MADAGASCAR HISSING COCKROACH

COFFEE

BLACK-AND-WHITE LEMUR

BLACK-AND-WHITE RUFFED LEMUR

MADAGASCAR POISON FROG

GREATER BAMBOO LEMUR

EDIBLE MANIOC

MADAGASCAR GECKO

SWEET POTATOES

TÔLANARO

Malagasy board game
FANORONA

ANTSIRABE ①

TSIRIBIHINA

VILLAGE

FIANARANTSOA

Tsaranoro Massif

ANDRINGITRA NATIONAL PARK ③

ISALO NATIONAL PARK

WHITE SITAKA

FOSSA

TILAPIA

②

COTTON

MANGOKY

RING-TAILED LEMUR

BEACH

AVENUE OF THE BAOBABS

CORN

thorny forests grow in the west, dry part of the island.

TOLIARA

ONILAHY

ZEBU

MORONDAVA

PACHYPODIUM ROSULATUM
known as the elephant's foot plant

BISMARCK PALM

CROSSING A HANGING BRIDGE ②

CLIMBING IN THE TSARANORO MASSIF ③

RICKSHAW ①

75

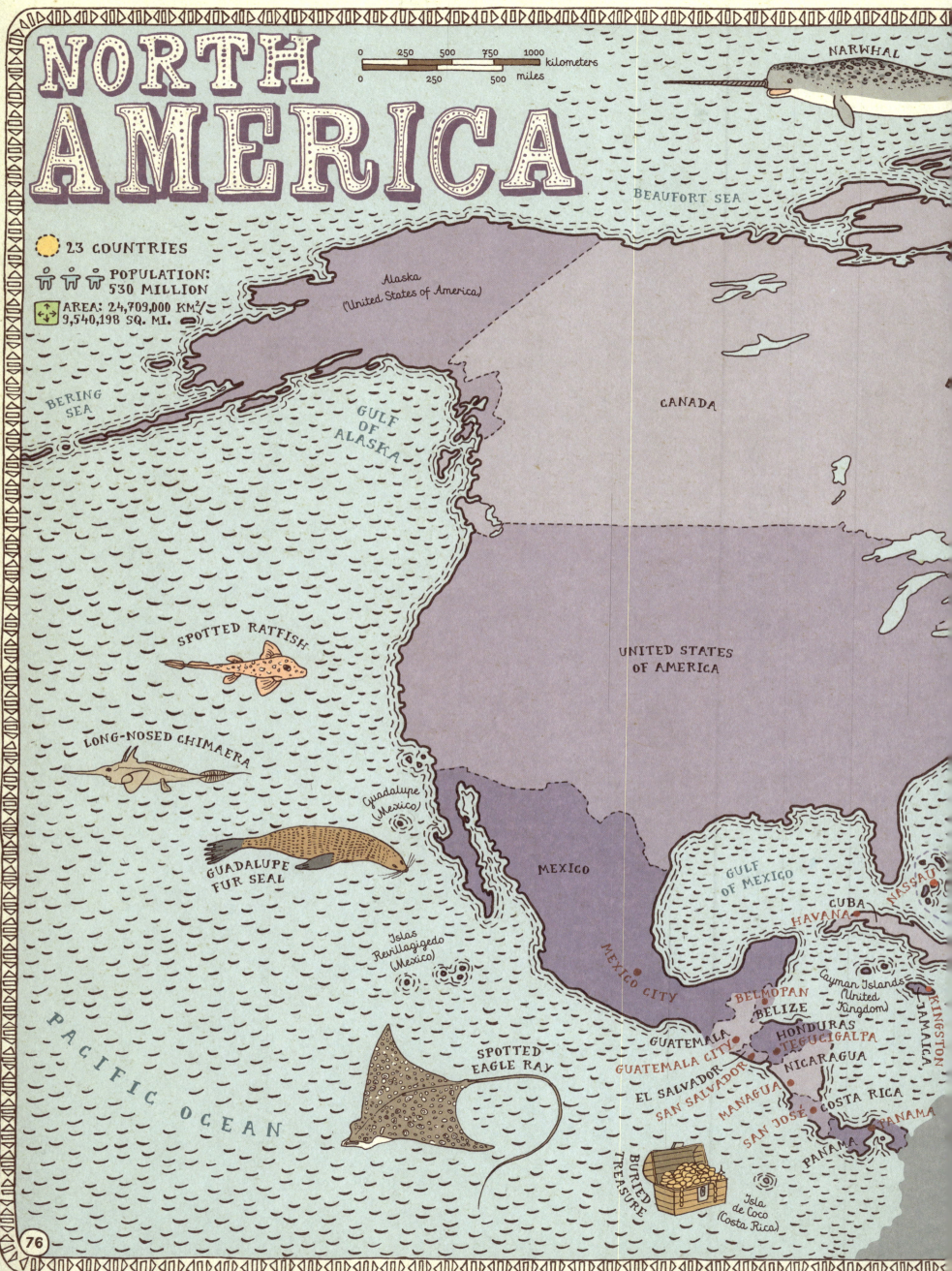

NORTH AMERICA

0 250 500 750 1000 kilometers
0 250 500 miles

23 COUNTRIES

POPULATION: 530 MILLION

AREA: 24,709,000 KM²/ 9,540,198 SQ. MI.

NARWHAL

BEAUFORT SEA

Alaska (United States of America)

BERING SEA

GULF OF ALASKA

CANADA

SPOTTED RATFISH

LONG-NOSED CHIMAERA

UNITED STATES OF AMERICA

Guadalupe (Mexico)

GUADALUPE FUR SEAL

Islas Revillagigedo (Mexico)

MEXICO

GULF OF MEXICO

MEXICO CITY

CUBA

HAVANA

NASSAU

Cayman Islands (United Kingdom)

BELMOPAN

BELIZE

HONDURAS

TEGUCIGALPA

JAMAICA

KINGSTON

GUATEMALA

GUATEMALA CITY

EL SALVADOR

SAN SALVADOR

MANAGUA

NICARAGUA

SAN JOSÉ

COSTA RICA

PANAMA

PANAMA

SPOTTED EAGLE RAY

PACIFIC OCEAN

BURIED TREASURE

Isla de Coco (Costa Rica)

GREENLAND
(Denmark)

BAFFIN
BAY

NUUK

GREENLAND WHALE

BELUGA WHALE

HUDSON
BAY

ATLANTIC OCEAN

OTTAWA

Saint-Pierre
and Miquelon
(France)

WASHINGTON, DC

Azores
(Portugal)

Bermuda
(United
Kingdom)

SARGASSO
SEA

CHRISTOPHER
COLUMBUS'S
SHIP

ROUTE OF
CHRISTOPHER
COLUMBUS'S
FIRST
VOYAGE

BAHAMAS
Turks and Caicos Islands (United Kingdom)
HAITI

PORT-AU-PRINCE
DOMINICAN REPUBLIC

PUERTO RICO (United States of America)
British Virgin Islands
United States Virgin Islands
Anguilla (United Kingdom)
Saint-Martin (France and Netherlands)
Saint-Barthélemy (France)

SAN JUAN

ANTIGUA AND BARBUDA
SAINT JOHN'S
Montserrat (United Kingdom)
Guadeloupe (France)
DOMINICA
ROSEAU
Martinique (France)
SAINT LUCIA
CASTRIES
BARBADOS
BRIDGETOWN
SAINT VINCENT AND THE GRENADINES
KINGSTOWN
SAINT GEORGE'S
GRENADA

SANTO
DOMINGO

CARIBBEAN
SEA

Aruba
(Netherlands)

Curaçao
(Netherlands)

Bonaire
(Netherlands)

PORT-OF-SPAIN
TRINIDAD
AND TOBAGO
BASSETERRE
SAINT KITTS
AND NEVIS

Saba
(Netherlands)

Saint Eustatius
(Netherlands)

① prospectors during the GOLD RUSH on the Klondike River

② JACK LONDON, American writer, who prospected for gold on the Klondike

TUFFED PUFFIN

CANADIAN TIMBER WOLF

ARCTIC OCEAN

WALRUS

CARIBOU

SNOW GOOSE

AMERICAN BLACK BEAR

United States of America (see pages 76-77)

BEAUFORT SEA

Banks Island

Victoria Island

YUKON

Alaska

SOCKEYE SALMON

●FAIRBANKS

JACK LONDON'S CABIN ②

MT. MCKINLEY 6,194 meters / 20,320 ft., the highest peak in North America

① DAWSON
MILES CANYON

MACKENZIE

GREAT BEAR LAKE

Northwest Territories

ANCHORAGE

FIRST NATIONS CARVINGS

MOUNTAIN GOAT

ESKIMO CURLEW

MT. LOGAN / 5,959 meters / 19,524 ft., the highest peak in Canada

●WHITEHORSE

closed-down gold mine

DIAMOND MINE

ST. NICHOLAS RUSSIAN ORTHODOX CHURCH JUNEAU

YELLOWKNIFE●

GREAT SLAVE LAKE

TIMBER PRODUCTION

PACIFIC OCEAN

RAINBOW TROUT

British Columbia

OIL DRILLING

LAKE ATHABASCA

Queen Charlotte Islands

ROCKY MOUNTAINS

Alberta

FORT EDMONTON HISTORICAL PARK

Peace

ATHABASCA

Saskatchewan

FLAX

RYE

CANADIAN BEAVER

LIONS GATE BRIDGE

EDMONTON

SASKATCHEWAN

OLIVIA   ETHAN

CANADIAN PORCUPINE

FIRST NATIONS TOTEM POLE IN STANLEY PARK ③

SADDLEDOME arena for hockey and lacrosse

④

Canada is the second largest country in the world (after Russia).

Vancouver Island

●VANCOUVER ③

●CALGARY ④

OATS

BARLEY

VICTORIA

CRAIGDARROCH CASTLE

The country's name is spelled the same in English and French.

← Canada

BANFF NATIONAL PARK ④

RED MAPLE

SASKAT... BERRIES

CANADA

⋀ CAPITAL: OTTAWA

👅 LANGUAGES: ENGLISH, FRENCH as well as Inuktitut and other First Nations languages

CANADA GOOSE

ROYAL CANADIAN MOUNTED POLICE

SUGAR MAPLE

♙♙♙ POPULATION: 34 MILLION

78 ⇕⇔ AREA: 9,984,670 KM²/ 3,855,103 SQ. MI.

0   250   500 kilometers
0   250 miles

BALSAM FIR

METEOROLOGICAL OBSERVATORY

Ellesmere Island

ALERT the northernmost permanently inhabited place in the world

Devon Island

POLAR BEAR

LACROSSE

BROOMBALL

ICE HOCKEY

JIGGS DINNER salt beef with potatoes, vegetables, and pease pudding

POUTINE French fries with cheese curd and gravy

BUTTER TART a pastry with a filling made of butter, eggs, and sugar

BAFFIN BAY

INUIT in traditional dress

FISHING

HARP SEAL

MUSK OX

Baffin Island

AUYUITTUQ NATIONAL PARK

TREKKING ACROSS SNOWY TERRAIN

MOOSE

PANGNIRTUNG

KAYAKING

Nunavut

INUKSUK traditional Inuit marker

IQALUIT

GREAT NORTHERN LOON

TUNDRA

TORNGAT MOUNTAINS NATIONAL PARK

ATLANTIC OCEAN

TAIGA

ARCTIC FOX

Newfoundland

HUDSON BAY

Québec

Newfoundland and Labrador

WAPUSK NATIONAL PARK

Manitoba

SOYBEANS

Labrador

MINGAN ARCHIPELAGO NATIONAL PARK RESERVE

Newfoundland Island

SUGAR SHACK

Nelson

RAPESEED

POLAR BEAR WATCHING

LIGHTHOUSE

ST. JOHN'S

WHEAT

MANITOBA LEGISLATIVE BUILDING

RED KNOT

MAPLE SYRUP

OKA CHEESE

CHÂTEAU FRONTENAC HOTEL

New Brunswick

CHARLOTTETOWN Prince Edward Island

Winnipegosis

Winnipeg

Ontario

CLOCK TOWER

Manitoba

CN TOWER 553 meters 1,815 ft.

QUÉBEC

HALIFAX Nova Scotia

CANOE

WINNIPEG

MEMBERS OF THE IROQOIS LEAGUE IN TRADITIONAL DRESS

NIPIGON

PARLIAMENT BUILDING

ST. LAWRENCE RIVER

ANNE OF GREEN GABLES, the heroine of Lucy Maud Montgomery's novel, lived on Prince Edward Island.

SUPERIOR

MONTRÉAL

OTTAWA

ST. JOSEPH'S ORATORY

AMERICAN LARCH

HURON

MICHIGAN

TORONTO MISSISSAUGA HAMILTON

ONTARIO

OLYMPIC STADIUM

ERIE

NIAGARA FALLS

RAVEN

SPACE NEEDLE

SEATTLE
Washington
MOUNT RAINIER

WAPITI

GRIZZLY BEAR

TEPEE
traditional Lakota dwelling used when hunting

BLACKFOOT
tribal member in traditional dress

WOLF

LAKOTA CHIEF CRAZY HORSE ②

PORTLAND
COLUMBIA

Oregon

HAZELNUT

Montana

North Dakota

SUNFLOWER

TIMBER PRODUCTION

BLUE JEANS

BISON

CRAZY HORSE MEMORIAL

DEVILS TOWER

SEQUOIA

Idaho

SNAKE

YELLOWSTONE NATIONAL PARK

Wyoming

South Dakota

MISSOURI

Sequoias are the world's tallest trees.

GEYSER

GREAT SALT LAKE

MOUNT RUSHMORE
The presidents' heads carved into the cliff are seven stories high.

Nebraska

GRAPEVINES

Mustangs are descended from horses brought to America by the Spanish conquistadors.

MUSTANG

SALT LAKE CITY

OIL WELL

PRAIRIE

GOLDEN GATE BRIDGE

SAN FRANCISCO

Nevada

Utah

ARCHES NATIONAL PARK

ROCKY MOUNTAINS

DENVER

Colorado

PIGS

TRAILER HOME

Kansas

CASINO

CLIFF PALACE
a settlement built by ancient Pueblo people

TAOS PUEBLO

PICKUP TRUCK

California

LAS VEGAS

GRAND CANYON

New Mexico

Oklahoma

HOLLYWOOD

LOS ANGELES

SAGUARO CACTUS

Arizona

JOSHUA TREE

CATTLE

SAN DIEGO

COYOTE

UFO

ROSWELL

COWBOY

DALLAS

PACIFIC OCEAN

GOLD PROSPECTORS

PUMA

BOXING
is a popular sport in the United States.

EL PASO

RIO GRANDE

Texas

COWBOY BOOT

NORTHERN ELEPHANT SEAL

STAGECOACH

SAN ANTONIO

Texas is the second biggest state after Alaska.

actress MARILYN MONROE

BASEBALL

CHEER-LEADER

FIRST MOON LANDING
IN 1969

Hawaii

HONOLULU

The first personal computers were produced in the United States.

MOON

THOMAS EDISON
inventor

BASKETBALL PLAYER

PACIFIC OCEAN

PINEAPPLE

MARY

JIM

EMILY

FOOTBALL

SHERIFF

80

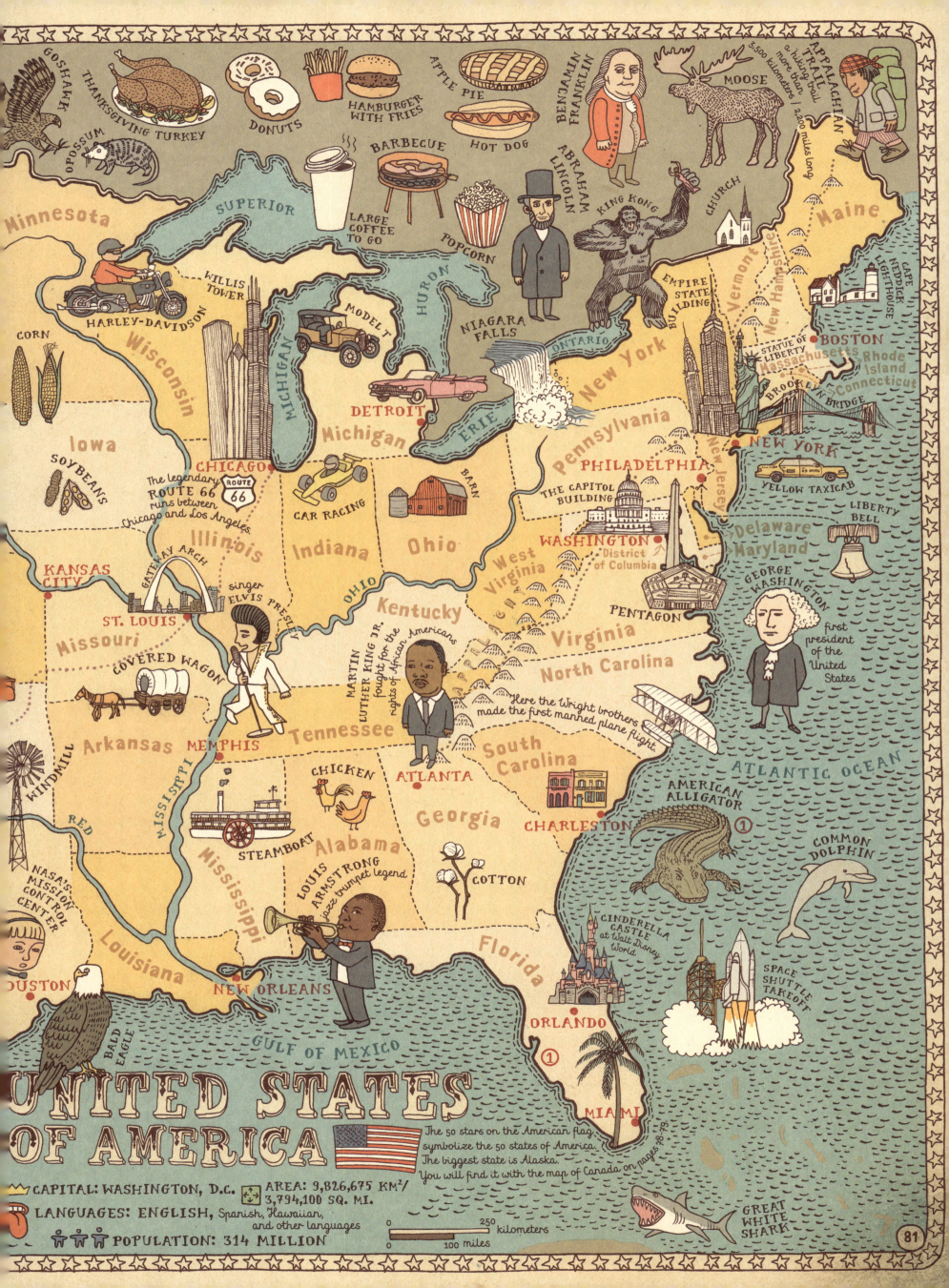

GOSHAWK

THANKSGIVING TURKEY

DONUTS

HAMBURGER WITH FRIES

APPLE PIE

HOT DOG

BENJAMIN FRANKLIN

MOOSE

APPALACHIAN TRAIL
a hiking trail more than 3,500 kilometres / 2,200 miles long

OPOSSUM

BARBECUE

LARGE COFFEE TO GO

POPCORN

ABRAHAM LINCOLN

KING KONG

CHURCH

MAINE

Minnesota

SUPERIOR

HURON

ONTARIO

EMPIRE STATE BUILDING

Vermont

New Hampshire

CAPE NEDDICK LIGHTHOUSE

WILLIS TOWER

MODEL T

NIAGARA FALLS

NEW YORK

STATUE OF LIBERTY

Massachusetts

BOSTON

Rhode Island

Connecticut

HARLEY-DAVIDSON

Wisconsin

MICHIGAN

ERIE

New York

Pennsylvania

BROOKLYN BRIDGE

CORN

DETROIT

Michigan

PHILADELPHIA

NEW YORK

YELLOW TAXICAB

LIBERTY BELL

Iowa

CHICAGO

ROUTE 66

CAR RACING

BARN

THE CAPITOL BUILDING

WASHINGTON
District of Columbia

Delaware

Maryland

SOYBEANS

The legendary ROUTE 66 runs between Chicago and Los Angeles.

Illinois

Indiana

Ohio

West Virginia

GEORGE WASHINGTON
first president of the United States

KANSAS CITY

GATEWAY ARCH

singer ELVIS PRESLEY

Kentucky

PENTAGON

ST. LOUIS

OHIO

MARTIN LUTHER KING JR. fought for the rights of African Americans

Virginia

North Carolina

Missouri

COVERED WAGON

Tennessee

Here the Wright brothers made the first manned plane flight.

WINDMILL

Arkansas

MEMPHIS

CHICKEN

ATLANTA

South Carolina

AMERICAN ALLIGATOR

COMMON DOLPHIN

RED

MISSISSIPPI

STEAMBOAT

Alabama

Georgia

CHARLESTON

ATLANTIC OCEAN

Mississippi

LOUIS ARMSTRONG jazz trumpet legend

COTTON

NASA'S MISSION CONTROL CENTER

Louisiana

CINDERELLA CASTLE at Walt Disney World

SPACE SHUTTLE TAKEOFF

HOUSTON

NEW ORLEANS

Florida

BALD EAGLE

GULF OF MEXICO

ORLANDO

MIAMI

GREAT WHITE SHARK

UNITED STATES
OF AMERICA

The 50 stars on the American flag symbolize the 50 states of America. The biggest state is Alaska. You will find it with the map of Canada on pages 78–79.

CAPITAL: WASHINGTON, D.C.

AREA: 9,826,675 KM² / 3,794,100 SQ. MI.

LANGUAGES: ENGLISH, Spanish, Hawaiian, and other languages

POPULATION: 314 MILLION

250 kilometers
100 miles

TIJUANA MEXICALI
EL PINACATE BIOSPHERE RESERVE
MEXICAN WOLF
PRICKLY PEAR CACTUS
CATHEDRAL
PRICKLY PEARS
PECCARY

CULTURAL CENTER
Sonoran Desert
SAGUARO CACTUS
CIUDAD JUÁREZ
SOUTH AMERICAN RATTLESNAKE
GOLDEN BARREL CACTUS

Sonoran Desert
Chihuahuan Desert
MILK SNAKE

OSPREY
Baja California
Angel de la Guarda
Tiburón
PAQUIMÉ ① the ruins of a pre-Columbian city

PREHISTORIC CAVE PAINTINGS
SIERRA MADRE OCCIDENTAL
BASASEACHIC FALLS

GULF OF CALIFORNIA
COPPER CANYON
CONCHOS

WHEAT
CATTLE
PUERTA DE TORREÓN

GRAY WHALE
WHALE WATCHING
COCONUT PALMS
LA PAZ
FARO lighthouse
GÓMEZ PALACIO
TORREÓN

SIERRA DE ÓRGANOS
SILVER MINES

CABO SAN LUCAS
MAZATLÁN
AQUEDUCT
ZACATECAS

PACIFIC OCEAN
MARIGOLDS
AGUASCALIENTES
CORN

THE AZTEC people dominated large parts of pre-Columbian America from the 14th to the 16th centuries.
FIN WHALE the largest marine mammal after the blue whale
BEACH
RÍO GRANDE DE SANTIAGO
HOSPICIO CABAÑAS
GUADALAJARA
LEÓN

AZTEC DEITY ③
PUERTO VALLARTA
LAKE CHAPALA

Mexico's capital, Mexico City, was once the site of the Aztec city of TENOCHTITLAN.
SOMBRERO
MONARCH
SUGAR CANE

México ← the country's name in Spanish
0 100 200 kilometers
100 miles

MEXICO

⌒ CAPITAL: MEXICO CITY

LANGUAGE: SPANISH and many indigenous languages

POPULATION: 115 MILLION

AREA: 1,964,375 KM² / 758,449 SQ. MI.

82

SANTIAGO MARÍA JOSÉ

① THE PRE-COLUMBIAN ERA is the time before Christopher Columbus arrived in America.

MEXICAN RED-KNEED TARANTULA

NINE-BANDED ARMADILLO

PRONGHORN

RACCOON

TORTILLA
a flatbread made with corn or wheat flour

TAMALE
stuffed dough made with corn flour and baked in corn husks

NACHOS

LA CALAVERA CATRINA
skeleton of an upper-class woman

CHILI PEPPERS

VANILLA

TACOS
a corn tortilla with meat, onion, and tomatoes

DIEGO RIVERA
painted enormous MURALS.

SKUNK

BURRITO
a tortilla made with wheat flour stuffed with beans, meat, and rice

a Mexican carrying the heart of a blue agave

PITIYA,
or 'dragon fruit'

SKULLS MADE OF SUGAR
a popular decoration on the Day of the Dead

commonly seen images on the Day of the Dead

BLUE AGAVE

The Mayans and Aztecs drank CHOCOLATE with vanilla and chili.

FARO DEL COMERCIO MONUMENT

Río Bravo del Norte (RÍO GRANDE)

BISHOPRIC PALACE

PUENTE DE LA UNIDAD

PIÑATA

LUCHA LIBRE
mexican wrestling

MARIACHI
a traditional Mexican band

MONTERREY

CERRO DE LA SILLA
(Saddle Hill)

SPANISH HOGFISH

SIERRA MADRE ORIENTAL

COTTON

SEA ANEMONES

CHERUBFISH

AVOCADO

GULF OF MEXICO

ANZAZÚ CHAPEL

DIVING
among coral reefs

SAN LUIS POTOSÍ

CRUDE OIL DRILLING

the oldest CATHEDRAL in mainland North America

PYRAMID OF THE MAGICIAN at UXMAL
a Mayan city

MÉRIDA

CANCÚN

TAMPICO

GUANAJUATO

PÁNUCO

PYRAMID OF THE NICHES at EL TAJIN
a city of the Totonac people

TORRE MAYOR

TEMPLE OF KUKULKAN AT CHICHÉN ITZÁ
- a Mayan city

Cozumel

JERÉTARO

CATHEDRAL

PYRAMID OF THE MOON at TEOTIHUACÁN

COLOSSAL STONE HEADS
made by the Olmec civilization

TULUM
ruins of a Mayan city

PALACE OF FINE ARTS

Yucatán

③ MEXICO CITY

ORIZABA
volcano
5,636 meters / 18,491 ft.
the highest peak in Mexico

PUEBLA

TEMPLE OF THE INSCRIPTIONS at PALENQUE
built by the Mayans

① THE MAYANS
inhabited the Yucatán peninsula. In the pre-Columbian era they built palaces and pyramids.

POPOCATÉPETL
volcano

LA QUEBRADA

ONIONS

BALSAS

CARIBBEAN SEA

Divers leap from 35-meter / 125-foot high cliff.

OAXACA

TOMATOES

COFFEE

USUMACINTA

②

ACAPULCO

the pre-Columbian ruins of MONTE ALBÁN

LEMONS

BLACK-HEADED SPIDER MONKEY

MAYAN WRITING

JAGUAR

SUNNY BEACHES

RAINBOW-BILLED TOUCAN

SOUTH AMERICA

- 12 COUNTRIES
- POPULATION: 392 MILLION
- AREA: 17,840,000 KM²/ 6,888,062 SQ. MI.

kilometers 0 250 500 750 1000

miles 0 250 500

Galápagos Islands (Ecuador)

DWARF SPERM WHALE

PACIFIC OCEAN

GIANT OARFISH

Sala y Gómez (Chile)

Easter Island (Chile)

Desventuradas (Chile)

San Félix

San Ambrosio

Archipiélago Juan Fernández (Chile)

Alexander Selkirk

Robinson Crusoe

SAWFISH

VENEZUELA

CARACAS

BOGOTÁ

COLOMBIA

QUITO

ECUADOR

PERU

LIMA

LA PAZ

BOLIVIA

CHILE

ARGENTINA

SANTIAGO

GEORGETOWN
PARAMARIBO
French Guiana (France)
GUYANA
SURINAM
CAYENNE

NURSE SHARK

Saint Peter and Saint Paul
Archipelago
(Brazil)

BRAZIL

Rocas
(Brazil)

Fernando
de Noronha
(Brazil)

A T L A N T I C   O C E A N

BRASÍLIA

Trindade
(Brazil)

Martim Vaz
(Brazil)

PARAGUAY

ASUNCIÓN

SOUTHERN
STINGRAY

SPERM WHALE

URUGUAY

MONTEVIDEO

BUENOS AIRES

Tristan da Cunha
(United Kingdom)

HAMMERHEAD
SHARK

Gough
(United Kingdom)

Falkland
Islands

South Georgia

PACIFIC OCEAN

Darwin

Wolf

MAGNIFICENT FRIGATEBIRD

Pinta

SEA LION

MARINE IGUANA

COCKLES

ESMERALDAS

GALÁPAGOS PENGUIN

Isabela

Marchena

Genovesa

MANGROVE forests along the coast are flooded with seawater at high tide.

COCOA FRUITS

CACTI

Galápagos Islands

GALÁPAGOS LAND IGUANA

LAVA LIZARD

COCOA BEANS

Santiago

Fernandina

MANGROVES

Santa Cruz

Santa Fe

San Cristóbal

Ecuador's biggest PORT

LIGHTHOUSE

RICE

DARWIN'S FINCH

BLUE-FOOTED BOOBY

FLIGHTLESS CORMORANT

MANTA

PAPAYA

GALÁPAGOS TORTOISE

Floreana

Española

TUNA

PANAMA HAT

COFFEE BUSH

RED-FOOTED BOOBY

SURFING

COFFEE FRUITS

the colorful district of LAS PEÑAS

PACIFIC OCEAN

HUMPBACK WHALE

SHRIMP

GUAYAQUIL

CATALINA

JAVIER

MARLIN

Puná

BANANAS

MACHALA

BANANA TRE

Ecuador
The country's name is spelled the same in English and Spanish.

RONDADOR
Ecuadorean national instrument

RED ROCK CRAB

Ecuador

CAPITAL: QUITO

LANGUAGES: SPANISH as well as Quechua and other indigenous languages

POPULATION: 15 MILLION

AREA: 283,561 KM²/ 109,484 SQ. MI.

Many Ecuadoreans love to play SOCCER.

TAMARILLO fruit that grows on trees and looks like a tomato

MAXILLARIA ORCHIDS

25   50 kilometers
0   25 miles

BEAUTIFUL BEACHES

MITAD DEL MUNDO is a monument near the EQUATOR, which is the line that divides the globe into the northern and southern hemispheres.

CULPEO

POISON DART FROG

GREATER ANI

TSÁCHILA PEOPLE
The men color their hair bright red with a dye made from the seeds of the ACHIOTE fruit.

COCOA TREE

CLOUD FORESTS are mountain forests that are often shrouded in mist.

FAMOUS MARKET IN OTAVALO

HUMMINGBIRD

MOUNTAIN TAPIR

ACHIOTE FRUITS

ESMERALDAS

CHURCH OF SAN FRANCISCO

OTAVALO

OPOSSUM

EQUATOR

The country name Ecuador comes from the Spanish word for EQUATOR.

PICHINCHA volcano

SANTO DOMINGO

CAYAMBE volcano

TOUCAN BARBET

QUITO

ANTISANA volcano

ROSE PLANTATIONS

QUECHUA GIRL IN TRADITIONAL DRESS

ILLINIZA volcano

NAPO

COFFEE BEANS

QUILOTOA

COTOPAXI volcano

KAYAKING

CRUDE OIL DRILLING

RUBBER TREE

a lake inside the crater of a volcano

CHIMBORAZO 6,308 meters 20,696 ft., highest peak in Ecuador

TENA

HOT SPRINGS

BARLEY

BAÑOS

TUNGURAHUA volcano

The eastern part of the country is covered in TROPICAL RAINFOREST.

The bark is cut to release a flow of rubber milk, known as LATEX.

CAPYBARA

EL ALTAR volcano

GUINEA PIG

WHEAT

ALPACA

LLAMA

THE DEVIL'S NOSE railway line runs up a mountain slope amid spectacular scenery.

SPECTACLED CAIMAN

CORN

PASTAZA

BALSA

BROWN WOOLLY MONKEY

CATHEDRAL

INGAPIRCA the remains of Inca buildings

MANIOC

CUENCA

SHEPHERDESS

RIVER RAFTING

CRAMER'S EIGHTY-EIGHT BUTTERFLY

CITY GATES

OCELOT

ANDEAN CONDOR

CINCHONA

VAMPIRE BAT
The bark of the cinchona tree contains an anti-malaria medicine.

SANCOCHO a soup made of manioc, bananas, peas, and corn

LOJA

TARANTULA

The bark of the cinchona tree contains an anti-malaria medicine QUININE.

AJI SAUCE made from hot peppers

PATACONES fried green bananas

CHUQUIRAGA

SPECTACLED BEAR

KING VULTURE

EYELASH VIPER

ECUADOREAN CEVICHE

FANESCA a fish soup made with many kinds of grains, eaten in Easter Week

POTATOES

RING-TAILED COATI

a dish of seafood, lime juice, tomatoes, onion, and herbs

87

Peru

Perú
the country's name in Spanish

〽 CAPITAL: LIMA

👄 LANGUAGES: SPANISH as well as Quechua, Aymara, and other indigenous languages

POPULATION: 29 MILLION

AREA: 1,285,216 KM²/ 496,225 SQ. MI.

CHILI PEPPERS

TOMATOES

PEANUTS

GOELDI'S MARMOSET

CUSTARD APPLE

MILITARY MACAW

PUMA

TAMANDUA

CORN

ANTICUCHOS grilled meat

HARPY EAGLE

a man in a PONCHO

RAINBOW BOA

CUPUAÇU

CHULLO TRADITIONAL QUECHUA HAT

HUATIA a traditional oven

PERUVIAN CEVICHE raw fish marinated in lemon juice with onion and chili

CHUPE DE CAMARONES shrimp soup

VICTORIA AMAZONICA

FESTIVE AMAZON PARROT

AMAZON

BELÉN floating village

YAVARÍ

QUECHUAN WOMAN AND C...

PERUVIAN GIANT CENTIPEDE

TAYRA

PUTUMAYO

NAPO

IQUITOS

PYGMY MARMOSET

PUCALLPA

YELLOW-FOOTED TORTOISE

Iquitos is accessible only by PLANE or BOAT.

EQUATORIAL RAINFOREST

ARAPAIMA

BLACK CAIMAN

UCAYALI

TARSIER LEAF FROG

SOCCER is the most popular sport in Peru.

PERIANDER METALMARK BUTTERFLY

PACA

PASTAZA

MARAÑÓN

HUALLAGA

COFFEE

ANDEAN COCK-OF-THE-ROCK

CANTUA BUXIFOLIA, known as the sacred flower of the Incas

a boy playing a SIKU

NORTHERN VISCACHA

LLAMAS

HUASCARÁN 6,768 meters / 22,205 the highest peak in Peru

CAJAMARCA

POTATOES

a man playing a CHARANGO

VICUÑA

statue from the pre-Columbian city of CHAN CHAN

TRUJILLO

CHICLAYO

COLONIAL ARCHITECTURE

CARLA SERGIO

QUENA

SULLANA

PIURA

ROYAL TOMBS OF SIPAN MUSEUM

CATHEDRAL

BEACH

100 kilometers
50 miles
50
0

COLLARED PECCARY

HOATZIN

MADRE DE DIOS

TARUCA

FLOATING ISLANDS home to the Uru people

LAKE TITICACA

JULIACA

PUNO

SANTA CATALINA MONASTERY

URU REED BOATS

TACNA

PREHISTORIC DRAWINGS IN TOQUEPALA CAVES

EMPEROR TAMARIN

MANÚ NATIONAL PARK

CATHEDRAL

WHEAT

EL MISTI volcano

AREQUITA

COTTON

CATTLEYA ORCHID

GUINEA PIG

MACHU PICCHU ruins of an Incan city

CUZCO

SUGAR CANE

PERUVIAN BOOBY

URUBAMBA

APURÍMAC

BARLEY

COLCA CANYON

HUMBOLDT PENGUIN

PERUVIAN FERN STICK INSECT

COCA

HUANCAYO

FLIGHT OVER THE NAZCA LINES

THE NAZCA LINES

NAZCA

YELLOWFIN TUNA

CORN

ICA

SOUTH AMERICAN SEA LION

HUÁNUCO

HUASCARÁN NATIONAL PARK

CHINCHA ALTA

HUARAZ

HUACHO

SAN FRANCISCO CHURCH

LIMA

GREAT WHITE SHARK

ROSEATE SPOONBILL

RICE

PERUVIAN TORPEDO

CORVINA DRUM

PERUVIAN ANCHOVETA

BONITO

PACIFIC OCEAN

SOUTH AMERICAN TAPIR

PICO DA NEBLINA
2,997 meters / 9,823 ft., the highest peak in Brazil

THREE-TOED SLOTH

BLUE-FRONTED PARROT

SHRIMP
one of the two longest rivers in the world (the other is the Nile)

PARÁ RUBBER TREE

AÇAI PALM

GOLIATH BIRDEATER SPIDER

NEGRO

YELLOW-BANDED POISON DART FROG

AMAZON THEATER

AMAZON RIVER DOLPHIN

MATA MATA

Marajó

AÇAI BERRIES

MANAUS

AMAZON

MADEIRA

BELÉM

COMMON SQUIRREL MONKEY

MAGNIFICENT HUMMINGBIRD

AMAZONIAN MANATEE

NEON TETRA

JAGUAR

A large part of Amazonia is covered in tropical rainforest.

PIRANHA

GIANT ARMADILLO

TOCO TOUCAN

XINGU

HYACINTH MACAW

ARAGUAIA

TOCANTINS

IRON ORE

GREEN ANACONDA

RED-AND-GREEN MACAW

TUFTED CAPUCHIN

DIAMONDS

CATHEDRAL

PARLIAMENT BUILDING

CUSTARD APPLE

ORANGES

BLACK BEANS

COYPU

BRASÍLIA

PINEAPPLE

GUARANA

YELLOW MOMBIN

GIANT ANTEATER

CATTLE

PARANÁ

SCARLET MACAW

PASSION FRUIT

BANANAS

GIANT OTTER

PIED TAMARIN

SÃO PAULO
the biggest city in Brazil

MARGAY

GOLDEN LION TAMARIN

IGUAZU FALLS

COFFEE

CURITIBA

BLACK HOWLER

HELICONIA

MANED WOLF

GREATER RHEA

CORN

SUNNY BEACHES

Many INDIGENOUS PEOPLE live in the Amazon rainforest.

BLUE-AND-GOLD MACAW

BOA CONSTRICTOR

BRAZILIAN PINE

SOYBEANS

RICE

PORTO ALEGRE

EDIBLE PINE NUTS

MANIOC

90

Brazil

Brazil has an excellent SOCCER team.

CAPOEIRA

Brazil is the fifth largest country in the world.

Brasil
↑
the country's name in Portuguese

⚑ CAPITAL: BRASÍLIA

LANGUAGES: PORTUGUESE as well as many indigenous languages

POPULATION: 200 MILLION

AREA: 8,514,877 KM²/ 3,287,612 SQ. MI.

0 — 250 kilometers
0 — 100 miles

MIGUEL   ISABELLA

Saint Peter and Saint Paul Archipelago

BROWN NODDY

JOSÉ DE ALENCAR THEATER

FORTALEZA

COMMON MARMOSET

LEAR'S MACAW

SUGAR CANE

Rocas

Fernando de Noronha

TUNA

FRASER'S DOLPHIN

BRAZILIAN THREE-BANDED ARMADILLO

RECIFE

SÃO FRANCISCO

ROLLED-UP THREE-BANDED ARMADILLO

CHURCH OF SÃO FRANCISCO

ACARAJÉ
stuffed, deep-fried bean croquettes

COCOA

SALVADOR

LIGHTHOUSE

ATLANTIC OCEAN

SHARPNOSE SEVENGILL SHARK

MANED SLOTH

BELO HORIZONTE

CABLE CAR to Sugarloaf Mountain

GREEN SEA TURTLE

SAMBA

38-meter / 125-foot-high STATUE of CHRIST THE REDEEMER

Trindade

Martim Vaz

SUGARLOAF MOUNTAIN

RIO DE JANEIRO ←

MARACANÃ STADIUM

A MAN IN TRADITIONAL DRESS

BRIGADEIRO
a chocolate cake

PÃO DE QUEIJO
cheese buns

FEIJOADA

SURFING

a man playing a CUÍCA drum

MOQUECA
a dish of seafood, onion, tomatoes, coconut milk, palm oil, and cilantro

a dish of black beans and meat served with rice, vegetables, oranges, fried manioc flour, and hot sauce

CARNIVAL DANCER

CHILE

- 🏔️ CAPITAL: SANTIAGO
- 👄 LANGUAGE: SPANISH and several indigenous languages
- 👥 POPULATION: 17 MILLION
- ⬜ AREA: 756,102 KM²/ 291,933 SQ. MI.

Chile
→ The country's name is spelled the same in English and Spanish.

A

N

D

Atacama Desert

① ATACAMA DESERT
Sometimes there is no rainfall here for many years.

① ATACAMA GIANT
an enormous drawing in the desert — 115 meters / 377 ft. long

SPACE OBSERVATORY

COPPER MINE

② OJOS DEL SALADO
6,892 meters / 22,664 ft.; the highest peak in Chile and the world's highest volcano

A CHILEAN IN CHAMANTO

PABLO NERUDA poet

GUANACO

DARWIN'S RHEA

CORN

LA MONEDA presidential palace

STRAWBERRIES

WINE

A MAPUCHE in traditional dress

③ SKIER

CATHEDRAL

SANTIAGO

VIÑA DEL MAR

VALPARAÍSO

PORT

COPIAPÓ

COQUIMBO

APPLES

ARICA

OLIVES

IQUIQUE

LOA

MANO DEL DESIERTO
an 11-meter / 36-foot-high sculpture by Mario Irarrázabal

ANTOFAGASTA

FUN AT THE BEACH

PERUVIAN PELICAN

HOUSES ON HILLS

ASCENSORES cliff railway in Valparaíso

CABLE CAR

BROWNINGIA CANDELARIS CACTUS

CHILEAN BELLFLOWER

CUECA DANCING

ANDEAN CONDOR

Desventuradas
San Félix
San Ambrosio

Archipiélago Juan Fernández

JUAN FERNÁNDEZ FIRECROWN

Robinson Crusoe

JUAN FERNÁNDEZ FUR SEAL

CRISTÓBAL CONSTANZA

SOCCER is a popular sport in Chile.

UGNI BERRIES

PINEAPPLE

HUMITAS
mashed corn flour boiled in corn husks

PASTEL DE CHOCLO
mashed corn baked with meat, olives, and hard-boiled eggs

POTATOES

EMPANADAS stuffed pastries

BEANS

QUINOA

CALDILLO DE CONGRIO
a soup made with sea eel

HUASO cattle-herder

100 kilometers
200
50 100 miles
0

PUMA

DEGU

CORURO

SOUTH ANDEAN DEER

ARAUCARIA CONE

DARWIN'S FROG

MONKEY PUZZLE TREE

KAYAKING

MACARONI PENGUIN

MAGELLANIC PENGUIN

VILLARRICA active volcano

LOS LAGOS REGION

DARWIN'S FOX

CHILEAN PUDÚ

TORRES DEL PAINE

Lake GENERAL CARRERA

E

S

P a t a g o n i a

CONCEPCIÓN

TALCAHUANO

TEMUCO

Bío-Bío

PUNTA ARENAS

CAPE HORN the southernmost point in South America

CHILEAN FLAMINGO

PUERTO MONTT

HOUSES ON STILTS

Chiloé

Dried seaweed is sold at market.

EDIBLE SEAWEED

GLACIER

SOUTH AMERICAN SEA LION

SURFING

SEA SNAILS

PATAGONIAN TOOTHFISH

CHILEAN DOLPHIN

FISHING BOAT

PINK CUSK-EEL

ORCA WHALE

SPINY DOGFISH

RED-TAILED TROPICBIRD

COMMON THRESHER SHARK

MASKED BOOBY

PACIFIC OCEAN

Sala y Gómez

PACIFIC OCEAN

BROWN NODDY

MOAI enormous statues produced many centuries ago by the inhabitants of Easter Island.

Easter Island

PACIFIC OCEAN

93

AUSTRALIA
AND OCEANIA

14 COUNTRIES

POPULATION: 36 MILLION

AREA: 8,536,716 KM²/
3,296,044 SQ. MI.

0 250 500 750 1000 kilometers
0 250 500 miles

MANDARINFISH

Wake
(United States)

Northern
Mariana
Islands
(United States)

THE MARIANA TRENCH
is an ocean trench almost
11 kilometers / 7 miles deep

Guam
(United States)

MARSHALL
ISLANDS

MICRONESIA

MAJURO

PALAU

NGERULMUD

PALIKIR

SOUTH
TARAWA

PAPUA NEW
GUINEA

NAURU
YAREN

K

SOLOMON ISLANDS

PORT
MORESBY

HONIARA

CORAL
SEA

VANUATU
VILA

AUSTRALIA

Coral
Sea
Islands
(Australia)

New Caledonia
(France)

Lord Howe
(Australia)

Norfolk
(Australia)

CANBERRA

CORAL REEF

GREAT AUSTRALIAN
BIGHT

TASMAN
SEA

NEW ZEALAND

LEAFY
SEADRAGON

Tasmania

94

Midway
(United States)

Hawaii
(United States)

HAWAIIAN MONK SEAL

PACIFIC OCEAN

Palmyra (United States)
Kingman (United States)

Howland
(United States)

Baker
(United States)

Jarvis
(United States)

K I R I B A T I

TUVALU
FUNAFUTI

Jokelau
(New Zealand)

Wallis
and Futuna
(France)

SAMOA APIA

FIJI

American
Samoa
(United States)

SUVA

TONGA

NUKU'ALOFA

Niue
(New Zealand)

Cook
Islands
(New Zealand)

Tahiti

French Polynesia
(France)

Pitcairn
(United
Kingdom)

CLOWNFISH

CROWN-OF-THORNS
sea star

YELLOW-BELLIED
SEA SNAKE

Kermadec
(New Zealand)

TIGER SHARK

WELLINGTON

Chatham
Islands
(New Zealand)

Bounty
(New Zealand)

BASKING
SHARK

AUSTRALIA

👑 CAPITAL: CANBERRA

👅 LANGUAGE: ENGLISH

🚶🚶🚶 POPULATION: 22 MILLION

✛ AREA: 7,741,220 KM² / 2,998,902 SQ. MI.

0 100 200 kilometers
0 100 miles

The rock paintings at Ubirr are thousands of years old.

TIMOR SEA

DARWIN

KAKADU NATIONAL PARK

DIDGERIDOO an Aboriginal wind instrument

NITMILUK NATIONAL PARK

Northern Territory

CAMELS were brought to Australia by 19th-century travelers.

BAOBAB

SPOTTED PYTHON

LILY

DAVID

PEARL CULTIVATION

BROOME

YELLOWTAIL AMBERJACK

Great Sandy Desert

SHORT-BEAKED ECHIDNA

ACACIA

EMU

WESTERN GRAY KANGAROO

BOOMERANG

ZEBRA FINCH

RED KANGAROO

INDIAN OCEAN

ABORIGINAL AUSTRALIANS are indigenous peoples of Australia.

KINGS CANYON

ALICE SPRINGS

KATA TJUTA

ULURU (AYERS ROCK) a sacred Aboriginal site

BUDGERIGAR

Western Australia

Great Victoria Desert

South Australia

AUSTRALIAN FOOTBALL

EUCALYPTUS

SCORPION

DINGO

AUSTRALIAN SEA LION

SUPER PIT gold mine

PAVLOVA meringue cake

PERTH

LITTLE PENGUIN

KING PRAWN

BANKSIA

GREAT AUSTRALIAN BIGHT

BLACK SWAN

MEAT PIE pastry with meat and tomato sauce

HUMPBACK WHALE

MACADAMIA NUTS

AUSTRALIAN PELICAN

VEGEMITE a spread made of yeast extract

WITCHETTY GRUB moth larvae, an Aboriginal snack

WINES

CRICKET

BARBECUE cooking meat on a grill

FRESHWATER CROCODILE

GREEN TREE PYTHON looped over a branch

Groote Eylandt

GULF OF CARPENTARIA

Mornington Island

SEA STAR

BARRAMUNDI

SEA WASP a toxic jellyfish

GIANT CLAM the world's biggest shellfish, can grow up to 1.5 meters / 5 feet

CORAL

COPPERBAND BUTTERFLY FISH

CASSOWARY

...SE-BREASTED COCKATOO

SULPHUR-CRESTED COCKATOO

GREAT BARRIER REEF

CORAL SEA

EASTERN GRAY KANGAROO

GLIDING POSSUM

SUGAR CANE

BLACK COAL

SEA ANEMONES

COCKATIEL

AUSTRALIAN GREEN TREE FROG

COTTON

BARLEY

REEF STONEFISH venomous fish

Queensland

LAKE EYRE

...ALS

LAKE TORRENS

KOALA

CATTLE

DIAMONDS

WHEAT

GREAT DIVIDING RANGE

SAND TIGER SHARK

TOWN HALL

BRISBANE GOLD COAST

SUPERB LYREBIRD

DARLING

New South Wales

RAINFORESTS

SURFING

SHEEP

WOOL

THE THREE SISTERS rock formation

BLUE MOUNTAINS

OPERA HOUSE

TASMANIAN DEVIL

GLENELG BEACH

ADELAIDE

MOUNT KOSCIUSKO 2,228 meters / 7,310 ft, Australia's highest peak

NEWCASTLE

SYDNEY

HARBOUR BRIDGE

Victoria

Kangaroo Island

MURRAY

PARLIAMENT BUILDING

Australian Capital Territory

CANBERRA

Tasmania

DUCK-BILLED PLATYPUS

FEDERATION SQUARE

LEATHERWOOD

HOBART

THE TWELVE APOSTLES rock columns

MELBOURNE

NEW ZEALAND

- 〰 CAPITAL: WELLINGTON
- 👄 LANGUAGES: ENGLISH, MĀORI, and New Zealand Sign Language
- 👥 POPULATION: 4 MILLION
- ⬚ AREA: 267,710 KM²/ 103,363 SQ. MI.

BUNGEE JUMPING

KING SALMON

TUATARA

SHEEP

KŌKAKO or NEW ZEALAND WATTLEBIRD

DIVER

SKY TOWER observation and radio tower

STONE STORE the oldest stone building in New Zealand

YACHTS

BEACH

THERMAL SPRINGS

Great Barrier

AUCKLAND

WAIKATO

HAMILTON

New Zealand's biggest lake

LAKE TAUPO

TROUT

RUAPEHU active snow volcano

WETA

LIGHTHOUSE

KAURI TREE

PUKEKOHE

North Island

WAITOMO GLOWWORM CAVES

GLOWWORMS

WHANGANUI

PŌHUTUKAWA

FLOWERS

RED-CROWNED PARAKEET

TUI

HECTOR'S DOLPHIN

TRADITIONAL MĀORI CANOE

MUSSELS

PURPLE PUKEKO, or SWAMPHEN

TASMAN SEA

Aotearoa
← or Land of the Long White Cloud, the country's name in Māori

SILVER FERN LEAF

SILVER FERN

50 100 kilometers
50 miles

ZORBING
spinning down a slope or on water inside a large ball

RUGBY

HEI-TIKI
Māori amulet

TĀ MOKO traditional Māori tattoos

HĀNGI
A traditional way of cooking meat and vegetables on heated stones in a pit covered with earth

KIWI

LOLLY CAKE
a cake with a filling made of sweets

HAKA
traditional Māori dance

BENJAMIN LILY

YAMS
sweet potatoes

meringue cake PAVLOVA

THE MĀORI
are the indigenous people of New Zealand.

HONGI
a Māori greeting, involving touching foreheads and noses

FISH AND CHIPS

edible HUHU grubs

MAGENTA PETREL

Chatham

Pitt

FORGET-ME-NOT

ERECT-CRESTED PENGUIN

Bounty Islands

CHATHAM ISLAND ROBIN

SPERM WHALE

PARLIAMENT BUILDINGS

ELECTRIC BUS

WELLINGTON

TE PAPA
National Museum of New Zealand

WHALE WATCHING

COOK STRAIT

KAHAWAI

PACIFIC OCEAN

NEW ZEALAND ROBIN

KEA

CHRISTCHURCH

MOERAKI BOULDERS
Large, spherical rocks

WHEAT

YELLOWHEAD

LARNACH CASTLE

ORANGE ROUGHY

GREAT SPOTTED KIWI

PUNAKAIKI PANCAKE ROCKS

ALPS

BARLEY

WAITAKI

SOUTHERN BROWN KIWI

DUNEDIN

YELLOW-EYED PENGUIN

NEW ZEALAND SEA LION

NEW ZEALAND SCALLOP

FOX GLACIER

MOUNT COOK (AORAKI)
3,764 meters / 12,349 ft., New Zealand's highest peak

SOUTHERN ALPS

CLUTHA

GRAPEVINES

YELLOW-CROWNED PARAKEET

Stewart Island

CABBAGE TREE

PĀUA SHELL

Secretary Island

MILFORD SOUND

WAIAU

TAKAHĒ

KAKAPO
Nightless parrot

Snares Islands

99

Rotuma

PINEAPPLE

CORN

BANANAS

GUAVA

DURUKA
a variety
of sugar cane

PEELED
DURUKA

COCOA

CEREMONY
FOR PREPARING
KAVA
– a drink made from
a species of pepper,
Piper methysticum

LOVO OVEN

Food is wrapped
in banana leaves
and cooked on hot stones
under a layer of earth.

TARO

GINGER

RICE

KOKODA
fish marinated with
lime, coconut cream,
tomatoes, and chili

Yasawa

TOBACCO

LALI
DRUM

Nacula

FIJI CRESTED
IGUANA

Yaduo

Vanua Levu

SHELLS

Navti

Yageta

NAVALA
VILLAGE

TUNA

COCONUT

TABUA,
a sperm whale tooth,
is a traditional gift

Waya

VILLAGE

Makongai

Wakaya

Viti Levu

BASKET
MADE OF
PALM LEAVES

BA

LAUTOKA

HINDU TEMPLE
AT NADI

TOMANIVI
1,324 meters / 4,341 ft,
Fiji's highest peak

Ovalau

LEVUKA

Batiki

TROPICAL
RAINFOREST

REWA

BEACH

SUGAR
CANE

PANDANUS

②

NAUSORI

SUVA

BASKET
WEAVING

BREADFRUIT

Bega

Vatulele

YELLOW
TANG

SURFING

Ono-i-Lau

NONI
FRUITS

MEKE,
TRADITIONAL
DANCE

CRIMSON SHINING
PARROT

FIJI
PARROTFINCH

DIVING

SEA STAR

Vatoa

CORAL
REEF

Kandavu

100

FIJI

edible TARO TUBERS

MANIOC

Cikobia

HIBISCUS

FIJI SNAKE

ORANGE FRUIT DOVE

👑 CAPITAL: SUVA

LABASA

FIJI ← The country's name is the same in English and Hindustani.

LANGUAGES: ENGLISH, FIJIAN, HINDUSTANI

Rabi

MATANITU KO VITI
↳ the country's name in Fijian

👥👥👥 POPULATION: 890 THOUSAND

↕ AREA: 18,274 KM²/ 7,056 SQ. MI.

0   25 kilometers
      10 miles

फ़िजी ← the country's name in Hindustani, written in Devanagari script

RUGBY

① Qamea

PACIFIC OCEAN

TAGIMAUCIA

Taveuni

BOUMA NATIONAL PARK

EPELI   LITIA

COCONUT PALMS

Vanua Balavu

Koro

BROWN BOOBY

KORO SEA

Mango

BANDED SEA KRAIT

Turuca

MAHIMAHI

Cicia

Nairai

HAWKSBILL SEA TURTLE

Nayau

Gau

FIJI BLUE DEVIL DAMSELFISH

DESERT ISLAND

PRESIDENTIAL PALACE GUARD

Lakeba

②

DRUA, TRADITIONAL BOAT

BUTTERFLY FISH

Moala

COLLARED LORY

PACIFIC OCEAN

Vuaqava

Namuka-i-Lau

lives only in Fiji

Totoya

FIJIAN MONKEY-FACED BAT

①

Kabara

Matuku

This very rare bat lives only on the island of Taveuni and feeds on fruit.

Fulaga

Ogea Levu

THE INUIT and YUPIK peoples are indigenous inhabitants of Alaska, Canada, Greenland, and Russia.

ICELAND GULL

GYRFALCON

THICK-BILLED MURRE

HORNED PUFFIN

BEARDED SEAL

Alaska (United States)

BEAUFORT SEA

SABINE'S GULL

INUIT SLED

LAKE ATHABASCA

GREAT SLAVE LAKE

WOLVERINE

GREAT BEAR LAKE

Banks Island (Canada)

Victoria Island (Canada)

ARCTIC WARBLER

RAVEN

WALRUS

RIDING A SNOWMOBILE

MUSK OX

ARCTIC WOLF

Devon (Canada)

Ellesmere Island (Canada)

ALERT

the northernmost settlement inhabited year-round.

Canada

HUDSON BAY

QAANAAQ

BAFFIN BAY

Greenland (Denmark)

RED-THROATED LOON

Baffin Island (Canada)

RAZORBILL

IQALUIT

HARP SEAL PUPS

IGLOO

INUIT TEPEE

HOODED SEAL

POLAR BEARS

NORTHERN GANNET

BELUGA WHALE

NUUK

PAAMIUT

TASIILAQ

ITTOQQORTOORMIIT

NARSARSUAQ

ATLANTIC OCEAN

THE ARCTIC

RIBBON SEAL

EAST SIBERIAN SEA

SNOWY OWL

New Siberian Islands

The Arctic is the region around the North Pole, the northernmost point on Earth. The North Pole is situated in the Arctic Ocean, surrounded by the Eurasian continent (meaning Europe and Asia) and North America.

LEMMING

TIKSI

LAPTEV SEA

RED PHALAROPE

PURPLE SAXIFRAGE

ROUGH-LEGGED BUZZARD

ARCTIC OCEAN

ARCTIC TERN

SNOW BUNTING

MOUNTAIN HARE

CHUKCHI WOMAN in traditional dress

Severnaya Zemlya (Russia)

ARCTIC FOX

REINDEER MOSS

ERMINE

North Pole

The North Pole is in the Arctic Ocean, which is almost always frozen over.

For most of the year, the Arctic is covered with SNOW.

SLED PULLED BY A REINDEER

DIKSON

Novaya Zemlya (Russia)

Franz Josef Land (Russia)

REINDEER

KARA SEA

NENETS PEOPLE in traditional parkas

NORD

ICEBERG

LITTLE AUK

LONG-TAILED DUCK

LONGYEARBYEN

Spitsbergen

Svalbard Archipelago (Norway)

BARENTS SEA

GREENLAND SEA

Bear Island (Norway)

MURMANSK

SAMI PEOPLE in traditional dress

Jan Mayen (Norway)

TROMSØ

Norway

Finland

Sweden

Russia

kilometers 0 100 200 300 400 500
miles 0 50 100 150 200 250

ANTARCTIC KRILL crustacea the size of a thumb which are eaten by birds, seals, and whales

SNOW PETREL

ANTARCTIC PEARLWORT

ANTARCTIC HAIR GRASS

HOURGLASS DOLPHIN

ROSS SEAL

ORCA WHALE

ANTARCTIC PENINSULA

WEDDELL SEA

No one lives in the Antarctic permanently. Scientists from various countries spend time at the numerous research stations. They come for several months or years to conduct scientific research.

Ronne Ice Shelf

WHITE-BLOODED FISH have transparent blood.

They do not freeze in very cold water.

An ice shelf is a platform of ice that is joined to the land and floats on the water.

VINSON MASSIF 4,892 meters / 16,066 ft. the highest peak in Antarctica

South Pole

AMUNDSEN-SCOTT SOUTH POLE STATION

ELLSWORTH MOUNTAINS

SOUTHERN ELEPHANT SEAL

EMPEROR PENGUINS are the world's biggest penguins.

Ross Ice Shelf

AMUNDSEN SEA

ROSS SEA

EREBUS active volcano

BLUE WHALE the biggest animal on Earth

SOUTHERN OCEAN

ANTARCTICA

○ 0 COUNTRIES

👤👤👤 POPULATION: 0

AREA: 14,000,000 KM²/ 5,405,430 SQ. MI.

The surface of the Antarctic is covered with snow and ice. The temperature here is below freezing all year round.

RESEARCH STATIONS

Lambert Glacier

In 1911, Norwegian ROALD AMUNDSEN led the first expedition to reach the South Pole.

A month later, a British expedition reached the Pole, led by ROBERT FALCON SCOTT.

Four kilometers / 13,000 feet under the ice, unfathomable and cut off from the world, lies LAKE VOSTOK

VOSTOK
Russian research station situated in the coldest place on Earth

TRANSANTARCTIC MOUNTAINS

ADÉLIE PENGUINS

GENTOO PENGUINS

ANTARCTIC COD

CRABEATER SEAL

SOUTHERN OCEAN

SOUTHERN ROYAL ALBATROSS

COLOSSAL SQUID

LEOPARD SEAL

WEDDELL SEAL

kilometers
0 100 200 300 400 500

miles
0 50 100 150 200 250

FLAGS OF THE WORLD

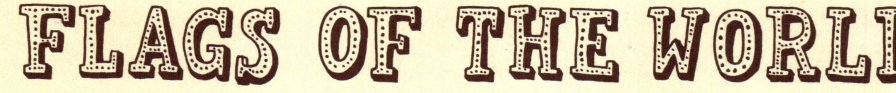

 Afghanistan	Albania	Algeria	Andorra	Angola	Antigua and Barbuda
Argentina	Armenia	 Australia	Austria	Azerbaijan	The Bahamas
Bahrain	Bangladesh	 Barbados	Belarus	Belgium	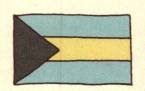 Belize
Benin	Bhutan	Bolivia	Bosnia-Herzegovina	Botswana	Brazil
Brunei	Bulgaria	Burkina Faso	Burma	Burundi	Cambodia
Cameroon	Canada	Cape Verde	Central African Republic	Chad	Chile
China	Colombia	Comoros	Democratic Republic of the Congo	Congo	Costa Rica
Croatia	Cuba	Cyprus	Czech Republic	Denmark	Djibouti
Dominica	Dominican Republic	East Timor	Ecuador	Egypt	El Salvador

Equatorial Guinea	Eritrea	Estonia	Ethiopia	Fiji	Finland
France	Gabon	Gambia	Georgia	Germany	Ghana
Greece	Grenada	Guatemala	Guinea	Guinea-Bissau	Guyana
Haiti	Honduras	Hungary	Iceland	India	Indonesia
Iran	Iraq	Ireland	Israel	Italy	Ivory Coast
Jamaica	Japan	Jordan	Kazakhstan	Kenya	Kiribati
North Korea	South Korea	Kosovo	Kuwait	Kyrgyzstan	Laos
Latvia	Lebanon	Lesotho	Liberia	Libya	Liechtenstein
Lithuania	Luxembourg	Macedonia	Madagascar	Malawi	Malaysia
Maldives	Mali	Malta	Marshall Islands	Mauritania	Mauritius

Mexico	Micronesia	Moldova	Monaco	Mongolia	Montenegro
Morocco	Mozambique	Namibia	Nauru	Nepal	Netherlands
New Zealand	Nicaragua	Niger	Nigeria	Norway	Oman
Pakistan	Palau	Panama	Papua New Guinea	Paraguay	Peru
Philippines	Poland	Portugal	Puerto Rico	Qatar	Romania
Russia	Rwanda	Saint Kitts and Nevis	Saint Lucia	Saint Vincent and the Grenadines	Samoa
San Marino	São Tomé and Príncipe	Saudi Arabia	Senegal	Serbia	Seychelles
Sierra Leone	Singapore	Slovakia	Slovenia	Solomon Islands	Somalia
South Africa	South Sudan	Spain	Sri Lanka	Sudan	Suriname
Swaziland	Sweden	Switzerland	Syria	Tajikistan	Taiwan